oliling uine

nnerigatoni

stoagnolotti

ellonishells

eesefarfalle

uladtortellini

the
pasta
book

Published by Fog City Press
814 Montgomery Street
San Francisco, CA 94133 USA

Chief Executive Officer: John Owen
President: Terry Newell
Publisher: Lynn Humphries
Managing Editor: Janine Flew
Art Director: Kylie Mulquin
Editorial Coordinator: Tracey Gibson
Editorial Assistant: Marney Richardson
Production Manager: Martha Malic-Chavez
Business Manager: Emily Jahn
Vice President International Sales: Stuart Laurence

Project Editors: Janine Flew and Anna Scobie
Project Designer: Jacqueline Richards
Food Photography: Valerie Martin
Food Stylist: Sally Parker
Home Economist: Valli Little

Library of Congress Cataloging-in-Publication Data

The pasta book.
        p. cm.
    Includes index.
    ISBN 1-876778-78-4
    1. Cookery (Pasta) I. Fog City Press.

  TX809.M17 P3534 2002
    641.8'22--dc21   2001054520

Color reproduction by Sang Choy International Pte Ltd

Manufactured by Kyodo Printing Co. (S'pore) Pte Ltd

Printed in Singapore

A Weldon Owen Production

the pasta book

FOG CITY PRESS

contents

a passion for pasta

Pasta: a simple Italian word for a simple food that has appeared on Mediterranean tables for centuries. In another form, known as noodles, it has been an Asian staple for even longer. Yet pasta has become so popular with cooks everywhere in recent years that it has also come to mean a world of good eating in almost any language.

Why has pasta been elevated from ethnic favorite to international culinary superstar? Probably because it fits in so well with today's cooking style. People want food that is light, easily prepared, and superbly fresh, made with the season's best offerings. Pasta's subtle flavor and slightly chewy texture make it a perfect partner for fresh vegetables and herbs. And not only is pasta good to eat and quick to prepare, it also provides a healthy bonus. Low in fat and high in carbohydrate, it plays an important role in a well-balanced diet. Another of pasta's advantages is that many dishes and sauces also freeze well, making the most of seasonal produce and providing easy meals at a moment's notice.

If long, thin spaghetti or tubular elbow macaroni are the pasta shapes that you are most familiar with, you are about to embark on a delicious voyage of discovery. *The Pasta Book* presents over 150 recipes from all over the world, showcasing fresh and dried pasta in all its variety, including the wonderful packaged fresh pastas widely available in supermarkets today.

In the pages to come you will be introduced to little bow ties known as farfalle, to pleated radiatori, to circular ruote with spokes like wagon wheels, to tight little twists called fusilli, and to many more, including new and tempting interpretations of classics such as tortellini, ravioli, and lasagne. You will also learn how easy and satisfying it is to make plain, whole-wheat, spinach, tomato, and herb pasta in your own kitchen.

The Pasta Book comprises two parts. Part One features recipes for vegetable, poultry, meat, and fish and seafood pastas, pasta salads, and recipes designed especially for the microwave oven. Part Two covers the basics of preparing homemade pasta and the best way to cook your own or purchased pasta so that it is served properly al dente. Useful tips appear throughout the book, from basic equipment needs to helpful hints to a glossary of ingredients.

So, whether you are preparing a simple family lunch or entertaining a crowd, you'll find something to suit your needs and please your palate. Try elegant Stuffed Pasta Rolls for a dinner party, or make a batch of Pumpkin and Bacon Rigatoni for a quick after-work meal. Plan Sunday lunch around Spaghetti with Creamy Clam Sauce, an update of the popular seafood dish, or Baked Pasta and Cheddar with Ham, a sophisticated version of a childhood favorite. With *The Pasta Book* at hand, you'll never be short of ways to make the most of this delicious, nutritious, and endlessly versatile ingredient.

part
One

recipes

vegetables, cheese, and nuts

poultry ❖ meat ❖ fish and seafood

pasta salads ❖ microwave

pasta *with* vegetables, cheese, *and* nuts

spiral pasta
with herbs

serves 4

13 oz (410 g) tortiglioni (large pasta spirals), rigatoni, or fusilli

3½ oz (105 g) butter, chopped

6 cloves garlic, finely chopped

1 cup (8 fl oz/250 ml) dry white wine

2–3 black peppercorns, crushed

chile powder, to taste

1 cup (1½ oz/45 g) combined finely chopped fresh mint, basil, and flat-leaf (Italian) parsley

salt and ground pepper

½ cup (2 oz/60 g) grated pecorino romano cheese

❖ In a large saucepan of boiling salted water cook the pasta until al dente; drain.

❖ Melt the butter in a large frying pan over medium heat. Add the garlic and cook, stirring, until it just begins to brown. Stir in the wine and cook until it evaporates. Stir in the crushed peppercorns.

❖ Add the pasta to the sauce mixture and stir in the chile powder and herbs. Season with salt and pepper to taste. Sprinkle with the cheese and serve.

sorrento-style pasta

serves 4–6

1¼ lb (625 g) ripe tomatoes, peeled,
seeded, and chopped

3 oz (90 g) black olives, pitted

⅔ cup (5 fl oz/160 ml) olive oil

1 clove garlic, finely chopped

a pinch of myrrh or dried
sweet cicely seeds

1 teaspoon dried oregano

1 cup (1½ oz/45 g) chopped
fresh basil

1¼ lb (625 g) fusilli (spiral pasta)

1¼ cups (5 oz/155 g) grated
Caciotta cheese

❖ In a bowl, combine the tomatoes, olives, olive oil, garlic, myrrh or cicely seeds, oregano, and basil. Set aside for at least 30 minutes, stirring occasionally to blend the flavors.

❖ Meanwhile, in a large saucepan of boiling salted water cook the pasta until al dente. Drain well, then add the sauce and cheese and toss to combine. Serve immediately.

shell pasta with vegetable sauce

serves 4

1 onion, thinly sliced

1 eggplant (aubergine), diced

4 tomatoes, cut into wedges and seeded

1 clove garlic, crushed

½ cup (4 fl oz/125 ml) olive oil

salt

1 green or yellow bell pepper (capsicum), diced

1 teaspoon dried oregano

3 oz (90 g) green beans, boiled until bright green and tender crisp

9½ oz (300 g) medium pasta shells

¼ cup (1 oz/30 g) grated Parmesan cheese

ground pepper

❖ In a large frying pan combine the onion, eggplant, tomatoes, garlic, and half of the oil. Cook until the onion softens. Season to taste with salt.

❖ In a saucepan heat the remaining oil. Add the bell pepper and oregano and cook, stirring, until soft. Add the bell pepper mixture and beans to the tomato mixture and cook for 5 minutes.

❖ Meanwhile, in a large saucepan of boiling salted water cook the pasta until al dente. Drain well. Add the vegetable mixture and the cheese and mix well. Serve sprinkled with pepper.

pasta norma style

serves 4

Norma **is the name of an opera written by Vincenzo Bellini, a native of Sicily. The Sicilians found his opera so inspiring that they often use the name "Norma" to describe anything they consider to be especially beautiful or good, such as this pasta dish.**

2 medium eggplants (aubergines)

coarse (kosher) salt

vegetable oil, for deep-frying

¼ cup (2 fl oz/60 ml) olive oil

2 cloves garlic, peeled and bruised

1 fresh chile, cut in half

1 lb (500 g) ripe tomatoes, peeled, seeded, and coarsely chopped

a few small fresh basil leaves

salt

13 oz (410 g) bucatini (hollow spaghetti)

¾ cup (3 oz/90 g) grated Parmesan cheese

❖ Slice the eggplants. Sprinkle the slices on both sides with coarse salt and place them in a colander to drain for 2–3 hours to rid them of their bitter juices. Wash the slices under cold water, then dry completely on paper towels.

❖ Deep-fry the eggplant in hot oil until golden; place on paper towels to drain.

❖ Meanwhile, heat the olive oil in a saucepan over medium heat. Add the garlic and chile and cook, stirring, until the garlic begins to brown. Remove the garlic and discard.

❖ Add the tomatoes and basil to the pan and season to taste with salt. Cook, stirring occasionally, for 20 minutes. Discard the chile halves.

❖ In a large saucepan of boiling salted water cook the pasta until al dente; drain.

❖ Place a layer of pasta in a large tureen. Add a few slices of fried eggplant, a little of the sauce, and sprinkle with cheese. Continue layering until all the ingredients are used. Serve immediately on warmed plates.

gnocchi
with cheese

serves 4

**This traditional Italian
dish uses fontina cheese,
a semi-firm cheese that
melts easily. Gouda or
Gruyère cheese can be
substituted, if desired.**

2 lb (1 kg) floury potatoes

1¾ cups (7 oz/220 g) all-purpose
(plain) flour, approximately

5 oz (155 g) fontina cheese, sliced paper-thin

2½ oz (75 g) butter, chopped

❖ Place the whole potatoes in a saucepan of cold salted water and bring to a boil. Cook until the potatoes are quite soft. Drain and quickly peel. While they are still hot, put the potatoes through a potato ricer or sieve held over a pastry board. Gradually work in the flour with your hands to make a soft, smooth dough. Continue kneading until the dough no longer sticks to your hands.

❖ Break off pieces of dough and roll out on the board using the palm of your hand, to make long sticks as thick as your little finger. Cut into ¾-inch (2-cm) lengths and place them on the board. Sprinkle with a little flour to prevent them sticking together. Press each piece lightly against the tines of a fork or the surface of a grater, while at the same time pushing down. This gives the gnocchi their characteristic shape.

❖ Preheat an oven to 475°F (230°C/Gas Mark 6). In a large saucepan of boiling salted water cook the gnocchi until they rise to the surface; drain. Arrange the gnocchi in layers in a buttered baking dish, placing the cheese between the layers. Dot the surface with the butter, then bake for 3–4 minutes. Serve immediately.

artichoke
ravioli

serves 3–4

PASTA

3¼ cups (13 oz/410 g) all-purpose
(plain) flour

3 eggs plus 2 egg yolks, beaten together

pinch of salt

1 egg, extra, beaten, for brushing

FILLING

8 small Italian artichokes

1 small leek, washed well, thinly sliced

3 tablespoons butter, melted

salt and ground pepper

2 tablespoons olive oil

2 eggs plus 1 egg yolk, beaten together

¾ cup (3 oz/90 g) grated Parmesan cheese

SAUCE

3 tablespoons butter, melted

pinch of fresh thyme leaves

❖ For the pasta, place the flour in a large bowl and make a well in the center. Add the eggs and salt and mix to form a dough. Roll the dough into a ball. Set aside, covered with a damp kitchen towel.

❖ For the filling, cut each artichoke into 4 wedges. In a frying pan, combine the artichokes, leek, half of the butter, salt, and pepper. Cook over low heat for about 15 minutes, then purée the mixture in a blender or food processor. Stir in the olive oil, eggs, and cheese.

❖ Roll out the pasta dough into 2 thin, 12-inch (30-cm) squares, and brush with beaten egg. Place the filling on 1 pasta sheet in ½-teaspoon portions, 2 inches (5 cm) apart. Top with the second pasta sheet and press down gently around each mound of filling. Use a ravioli wheel or fluted pastry wheel to cut into 2-inch (5-cm) square ravioli. In a large saucepan of boiling salted water cook the ravioli until they rise to the surface; drain well.

❖ For the sauce, combine the melted butter and thyme. Serve spooned over the hot ravioli.

recipe **hint**

Italian artichokes are very small and can be eaten whole, unlike most other varieties of artichoke. If you are unable to find them, use canned or thawed, frozen artichoke hearts, cut into bite-sized pieces.

pasta
with red wine, green onion, and zucchini sauce

serves 3–4

If you are short on time, you can use 13 oz (410 g) of any purchased short pasta in this recipe. Penne, farfalle (bow-tie pasta), and fusilli (spiral pasta) all work well.

PASTA

3¼ cups (13 oz/410 g) all-purpose (plain) flour

4 eggs

SAUCE

2 small zucchini (courgettes)

salt

2½ oz (75 g) butter

2 green (spring) onions, chopped

½ cup (4 fl oz/125 ml) beef stock

¾ cup (6 fl oz/185 ml) dry red wine

⅓ cup (1⅓ oz/40 g) grated Parmesan cheese

❖ Place the flour in a large mixing bowl and make a well in the center. Add the eggs and mix to form a dough. Roll out into a thin sheet and use a pastry cutter to cut into 2-inch (5-cm) squares. Roll each square around the handle of a wooden spoon and then roll over a pasta comb (a rectangular wooden frame about 8 x 4 inches [20 x 10 cm] with fine wooden strips across it positioned very close together). This will create classic ridged macaroni. If you do not have a pasta comb, you can roll the pasta over a cylindrical grater.

❖ Thinly slice the zucchini, sprinkle with salt, and place in a colander for 30 minutes. Rinse and dry well. Melt 3 tablespoons of the butter in a saucepan. Add half of the green onions, the stock, and wine. Cook over low heat until heated through. In a frying pan heat the remaining butter and briefly cook the remaining green onions and the zucchini.

❖ In a large saucepan of boiling salted water cook the pasta until al dente, about 5 minutes. Drain well. Add the pasta and cheese to the wine sauce and mix well. Serve immediately, topped with the zucchini mixture.

linguine
with almond and avocado sauce

serves 4–6

½ cup (4 fl oz/125 ml) plus
2 tablespoons olive oil

2 medium onions, diced

2 cloves garlic, chopped

salt and ground pepper

½ cup (¾ oz/20 g) shredded
fresh basil leaves

1 cup (3½ oz/100 g) almonds,
roughly chopped

2 medium avocados, peeled,
stone removed, mashed

juice of 1 large lemon

1 lb (500 g) linguine

❖ In a frying pan heat the 2 tablespoons of olive oil over medium heat, add the onions, and cook, stirring often, until translucent. Stir in garlic and salt, cover, and cook over low heat until soft.

❖ In a food processor combine the onion mixture, basil, almonds, avocado, and pepper. While the motor is running, gradually add the remaining ½ cup (4 fl oz/125 ml) olive oil and the lemon juice. Process until the mixture is smooth.

❖ In a large saucepan of boiling salted water cook the pasta until al dente. Gently warm the sauce just before the pasta is done and then stir into the hot pasta. Serve immediately.

rigatoni
in lemon cream sauce

serves 6

1¼ lb (625 g) rigatoni

1 cup (8 fl oz/250 ml) heavy (double) cream

¼ cup (2 oz/60 g) butter

grated zest (rind) of 2 lemons

1 cup (4 oz/125 g) grated Parmesan cheese

❖ In a large saucepan of boiling salted water cook the pasta until al dente. Meanwhile, in a small saucepan heat the cream, butter, lemon zest, and cheese.

❖ Drain the pasta, add the sauce, and mix well. Serve immediately.

chestnut ravioli
in mascarpone sauce

serves 4

Chestnuts are round, white nuts that are encased in a shiny, red-brown outer shell. They contain very little fat and can be boiled, steamed, braised, or roasted. Here, they are combined with ricotta to make a delectable filling for ravioli.

RAVIOLI

6 oz (185 g) chestnuts in their shells

6 oz (185 g) ricotta cheese

pinch of salt

pinch of grated nutmeg

pinch of ground rosemary

3¼ cups (13 oz/410 g) all-purpose (plain) flour

4 eggs

SAUCE

6 oz (185 g) mascarpone

3 fresh sage leaves

❖ For the ravioli, make a cut in each chestnut shell with a sharp knife, then cook in boiling water for 45 minutes. Drain; remove the shells and internal skins.

❖ In a blender or food processor process the nuts, ricotta, salt, nutmeg, and rosemary until smooth.

❖ Place the flour in a large mixing bowl and make a well in the center. Add the eggs and mix to form a dough. Roll out into a thin sheet and cut into 4-inch (10-cm) wide strips. Place the filling along 1 side of each sheet in 1/2-teaspoon portions, 2 inches (5 cm) apart. Fold each strip lengthwise back over the filling, pressing well around each mound. Use a ravioli wheel or fluted pastry wheel to cut out the ravioli. In a large saucepan of boiling salted water cook the ravioli until they rise to the surface; drain well.

❖ Meanwhile, for the sauce, place the mascarpone and sage in the top of a double boiler over simmering water. Beat with a wooden spoon until the mascarpone has a liquid consistency. Serve spooned over the ravioli.

recipe hint

If fresh chestnuts are unavailable, you can use canned or bottled chestnuts. Ensure that they are packed in water as opposed to a flavored syrup. Chestnut purée cannot be substituted.

tagliatelle
with mushrooms

serves 3–4

Porcini mushrooms, with their plump, swollen stems and intensely rich flavor, are highly regarded among food-lovers. In this recipe, they are combined with garlic and parsley to make a luxurious pasta sauce.

2²/₃ cups (9¹/₂ oz/305 g) all-purpose (plain) flour, plus extra for sprinkling

2 eggs plus 2 egg yolks, beaten together

¹/₂ cup (4 fl oz/125 ml) olive oil

salt

1 tablespoon butter

1 clove garlic, peeled and bruised

6¹/₂ oz (200 g) porcini (cèpes or boletus) mushrooms, stems removed, thinly sliced

1 sprig fresh flat-leaf (Italian) parsley, chopped

ground pepper

❖ Place the flour on a work surface and make a well in the center. Add the eggs, 2 tablespoons of the olive oil, and a pinch of salt and mix to a soft, smooth dough. Roll out into a very thin sheet. Roll up the sheet and use a sharp knife to cut into tagliatelle no more than ¼-inch (6-mm) wide. Lay the pasta out on the board, sprinkle with flour, and set aside for 1 hour to dry.

❖ In a frying pan combine the remaining oil, the butter, and garlic. Cook until the garlic browns, then discard the garlic. Add the mushrooms and cook, stirring, until browned. Season with salt, to taste.

❖ Meanwhile, in a large saucepan of boiling salted water cook the pasta until al dente; drain. Add to the frying pan with the parsley and cook, stirring, for 30 seconds. Season with pepper just before serving.

recipe variations

The stems from the porcini mushrooms can be kept to use when making stock. If porcini mushrooms are unavailable, you can use virtually any mushrooms to make the sauce, although you will not get the same intense flavor that porcini mushrooms deliver. Increase the quantity, if you like, to compensate for the more subtle flavor.

fettuccine
with bell pepper sauce

serves 4

*1½ lb (750 g) red and yellow
bell peppers (capsicums)*

⅓ cup (2½ fl oz/80 ml) olive oil

2 cloves garlic, finely chopped

1 teaspoon capers, drained

6 black olives, pitted

2 tomatoes, peeled

salt and ground pepper

9½ oz (295 g) fettuccine

*½ cup (2 oz/60 g) grated
Parmesan cheese*

❖ Remove the seeds and membranes from the bell peppers and cut into very thin strips. In a large frying pan heat the oil over low heat. Add the garlic and cook, stirring, for 1 minute. Add the bell peppers and cook, stirring often, until they soften.

❖ Add the capers, olives, and tomatoes and season to taste with salt and pepper. Cook, stirring, until the ingredients are well combined and heated through.

❖ In a large saucepan of boiling salted water cook the pasta until al dente; drain. Add the pasta to the frying pan and toss to combine. Serve sprinkled with cheese.

penne
with mushroom and tarragon sauce

serves 4

3 tablespoons butter

8 oz (250 g) small white (button) mushrooms

1 clove garlic, crushed

2 teaspoons fresh tarragon, finely chopped

salt and ground black pepper

1¼ cups (10 fl oz/310 ml) heavy (double) cream

1 teaspoon grated lemon zest (rind)

½ cup (2 oz/60 g) grated Parmesan cheese

1 lb (500 g) penne

❖ Melt the butter in a large frying pan. Add the mushrooms and cook, stirring, for 1 minute. Add the garlic and cook, stirring, for 30 seconds. Add the tarragon, salt, pepper, cream, and lemon zest. Stir over low heat for 2 minutes. Add the cheese and cook gently for 3 minutes, or until the mixture thickens slightly.

❖ Meanwhile, in a large saucepan of boiling salted water cook the pasta until al dente; drain. Add to the frying pan and stir to combine. Serve immediately.

ravioli with marjoram sauce

serves 4

PASTA

3¼ cups (13 oz/410 g) all-purpose (plain) flour

4 eggs, beaten

½ cup (4 fl oz/125 ml) water

2 tablespoons olive oil

pinch of salt

1 egg, extra, beaten, for brushing

FILLING

9 oz (280 g) ricotta

5 oz (155 g) cooked, well-drained spinach

2 eggs

½ cup (2 oz/60 g) grated Parmesan cheese

pinch of grated nutmeg

salt and ground pepper

SAUCE

¾ cup (3¾ oz/115 g) pine nuts

¼ cup (2 fl oz/60 ml) extra virgin olive oil

2 cups (3 oz/90 g) fresh marjoram leaves

2 cups (2 oz/60 g) fresh basil leaves

3½ oz (105 g) butter

salt

❖ For the pasta, heap the flour on a work surface and make a well in the center. Add the eggs, water, olive oil, and salt and mix to a smooth dough. Roll the dough into a ball and set aside, covered with a damp kitchen towel.

❖ For the filling, put the ricotta and spinach through a food mill, adding the eggs, cheese, nutmeg, salt, and pepper. Mix well.

❖ Roll out the dough into 2 thin sheets, each 12 inches (30 cm) square, and brush with the extra beaten egg. Place the filling on 1 pasta sheet in ½-teaspoon amounts, 2 inches (5 cm) apart. Top with the second sheet and press down gently around each mound of filling. Use a ravioli wheel or fluted pastry wheel to cut out 2-inch (5-cm) square ravioli.

❖ For the sauce, in a blender or food processor combine the pine nuts, 1 tablespoon of the olive oil, the marjoram, and basil. Blend or process until smooth. Transfer to a large, shallow frying pan and add the remaining olive oil, butter, and salt to taste. Stir until well combined.

❖ Meanwhile, in a large saucepan of boiling salted water cook the ravioli until they rise to the surface; drain. Add the ravioli to the sauce and stir to combine. Serve immediately.

agnolotti
filled with cheeses

serves 4–6

PASTA

4 cups (1 lb/500 g) all-purpose (plain) flour

2 eggs plus 2 egg yolks, beaten together

1 tablespoon olive oil

pinch of salt

FILLING

1 tablespoon butter

1 small onion, chopped

3 tablespoons ricotta cheese

3 tablespoons finely diced semi-firm cheeses, such as fontina, Montasio, or a combination of cheeses

2 tablespoons fresh goat's cheese

1 tablespoon fresh marjoram leaves

2 pinches of fresh thyme leaves

pinch of grated nutmeg

salt and ground pepper

SAUCE

3 oz (90 g) fresh porcini (cèpes or boletus) mushrooms, stems removed, thinly sliced

3 oz (90 g) butter, melted

✥ For the pasta, place the flour in a large mixing bowl and make a well in the center. Add the eggs, olive oil, and salt and mix to a smooth dough. Roll into a ball and set aside, covered with a damp kitchen towel.

✥ For the filling, in a small frying pan melt the butter over low heat. Add the onion and cook, stirring often, until it softens. Stir in the ricotta, semi-firm cheeses, goat's cheese, marjoram, and thyme until well combined. Add nutmeg and salt and pepper to taste.

✥ Roll out the dough into 2 thin sheets, each 12 inches (30 cm) square. Place the filling on 1 pasta sheet in ½-teaspoon amounts, 2 inches (5 cm) apart. Top with the second sheet and press down gently around each mound of filling. Use a ravioli wheel or fluted pastry wheel to cut out 2-inch (5-cm) square agnolotti. In a large saucepan of boiling salted water cook the agnolotti until they rise to the surface; drain.

✥ For the sauce, combine the raw mushrooms and melted butter. Serve spooned over the agnolotti.

recipe variations

Semi-firm cheeses are uncooked pressed cheeses that are ripened for a fairly long period of time in cool and very humid conditions. Dense and usually pale yellow in color, this category also includes cheeses such as Cheddar, Gouda, Gruyère, Edam, and Monterey Jack.

herbed oils and infusions

The olive oils of southern France and northern Italy are as varied and distinct in flavor as their wines, and almost as renowned. However, there are now also high-quality olive oils being pressed in Greece, Spain, southern California, and parts of Australia. Walnut, almond, and hazelnut oils can also be used to add their own distinctive, delicate flavor to salads and dressings, while sesame oil gives dishes a delicious Oriental flavor.

Tasting oils is like sampling wines. For a clear, true sample, dip a piece of white bread in the oil and taste. Let your personal preference be your guide. Extra virgin olive oil (made from the first pressing of the olives) has a low acidity and is the best quality olive oil. Generally, good-quality oils will keep, unopened, in a cool, dark place for about 2 years. Once opened, keep in a cool, dark place as before, but use within 6 months. Herbed oil infusions are ideal as a simple pasta sauce, for basting broiled (grilled) meats, for stir-frying vegetables, or to add to soups or salad dressings.

sterilizing jars and bottles

Fill a glass jar or bottle with boiling water and set aside for 10 minutes. Pour out the water and turn the jar or bottle upside down on a clean kitchen towel. Allow to dry thoroughly before using.

herbed olive oil

6 black peppercorns

6 sprigs fresh rosemary

3 bay leaves

2 sprigs fresh thyme

2 sprigs fresh oregano

4 cups (32 fl oz/1 liter) extra virgin olive oil

❖ Place the peppercorns and herbs in a sterilized 4-cup (32-fl oz/1-liter) bottle.

❖ Add the olive oil, ensuring all the herbs are completely covered.

❖ Seal, label, and store in the refrigerator for 10 days to infuse. This oil should be refrigerated throughout all stages of production. Keeps for up to 1 month.

makes 4 cups (32 fl oz/1 liter)

herbed oil infusion

1 cup (1 oz/30 g) fresh basil
or other herb leaves, well washed and dried

1 cup (8 fl oz/250 ml) extra virgin olive oil

1 sprig fresh basil or other herb,
for decoration (optional)

❖ Place the basil in a sterilized jar. Add the oil, ensuring the basil is completely covered.

❖ Seal and store in the refrigerator for 2–3 weeks. Taste after 2 weeks to check the intensity of flavor.

❖ Strain the oil into a sterilized bottle through a funnel lined with cheesecloth (muslin); discard the basil.

❖ A clean, dry sprig of fresh basil can be added to the oil to decorate, if desired.

❖ Seal, label, and store. This oil should be refrigerated throughout all stages of production. Keeps for up to 1 month.

makes 1 cup (8 fl oz/250 ml)

fresh herb pasta

serves 4–6

This dish makes a good accompaniment for veal or can be served on its own as an appetizer. The pasta is so tasty that it only needs a very light sauce and sprinkling of cheese.

1 quantity Semolina Pasta (pages 306–307)

½ cup (½–⅔ oz/15–20 g) each of cilantro (fresh coriander), dill, and flat-leaf (Italian) parsley leaves, washed and dried

⅓ cup (2½ fl oz/80 ml) olive oil

3 cloves garlic, finely chopped

2 tablespoons finely chopped fresh flat-leaf (Italian) parsley, extra

ground pepper

shavings of Parmesan cheese, for garnish

❖ Divide the pasta dough into 3 portions. Cover 2 portions with plastic wrap to prevent them from drying out. On a lightly floured surface, or using a pasta machine, roll out the remaining portion into a thin sheet. Scatter a third of each of the herbs over half of the sheet. Carefully flatten the herbs. Lightly brush the other half of the pasta sheet with water and fold it over to cover the herbs. Press down firmly to enclose the herbs and force out any air bubbles.

❖ Roll the folded sheet once more to make a very thin sheet of pasta. Use a sharp knife or pasta cutter to cut the sheet into 2-inch (5-cm) squares. Repeat the process with the remaining dough portions and herbs.

❖ In a large saucepan of boiling salted water cook the pasta until al dente; drain.

❖ Heat the oil in a frying pan. Add the garlic and cook gently, stirring, for 1 minute. Add the extra parsley and pepper and stir to combine.

❖ Add the pasta to the frying pan and toss to combine. Serve immediately, garnished with shavings of Parmesan cheese.

fettuccine
with broccoli and mustard

serves 6 as an appetizer

½ cup (4 oz/125 g) butter, softened

1 tablespoon strong Dijon mustard

3 green (spring) onions, finely diced

2 cloves garlic, crushed

2 tablespoons roughly chopped fresh
flat-leaf (Italian) parsley

2 teaspoons fresh tarragon leaves

1 lb (500 g) broccoli,
broken into small florets

8 oz (250 g) fettuccine or other ribbon pasta

¾ cup (6 fl oz/180 ml) crème fraîche
or light sour cream

2 tablespoons sliced sun-dried tomatoes

grated zest (rind) of 1 lemon

salt and ground black pepper

1½ oz (45 g) sliced (flaked)
almonds, toasted

❖ In a food processor, combine the butter, mustard, green onions, garlic, parsley, and tarragon. Process until well combined.

❖ In a large saucepan of boiling salted water cook the broccoli until bright green and tender crisp. Use a slotted spoon to remove from the pan. Add the pasta to the boiling water and cook until al dente; drain.

❖ Meanwhile, bring the mustard mixture to a boil over low heat. Boil for 1–2 minutes. Stir in the crème fraîche or sour cream, sun-dried tomatoes, and lemon zest. Heat through but do not boil. Stir in the broccoli. Season with salt and pepper. Spoon over the pasta and serve topped with almonds.

whole-grain spaghetti
with red cabbage and goat's cheese

serves 6 as an appetizer

1 tablespoon walnut oil

2 tablespoons olive oil

1 cup (4 oz/125 g) walnuts, chopped

1 clove garlic, chopped

2 tablespoons balsamic vinegar

1 red (Spanish) onion, thinly sliced

½ small red cabbage, finely shredded

salt and ground black pepper

1 green apple, cut into thin strips

1 tablespoon finely chopped fresh
flat-leaf (Italian) parsley

8 oz (250 g) whole-grain
(wholemeal) spaghetti

3½ oz (105 g) goat's cheese

❖ Heat the oils in a frying pan and cook the walnuts, stirring, for 2 minutes. Use a slotted spoon to transfer walnuts to paper towel to drain. Add the garlic and vinegar to the oil in the pan; stir to combine. Add the onion and cook, stirring, for 30 seconds. Add the cabbage and cook, stirring, until wilted. Season to taste with salt and pepper. Add the apple and parsley and stir well. Stir in half of the walnuts.

❖ Meanwhile, in a large saucepan of boiling salted water cook the pasta until al dente; drain. Crumble cheese over pasta, add cabbage mixture, and gently toss. Serve with remaining walnuts.

asparagus
tortellini

serves 4

This is an elegant modern version of a traditional Italian dish. Instead of the usual tortellini fillings, asparagus is used to complement the sauce.

FILLING

6 oz (185 g) asparagus tips

3 oz (90 g) ricotta cheese

½ cup (2 oz/60 g) grated Parmesan cheese

3 tablespoons heavy (double) cream

salt and ground pepper

PASTA

2½ cups (10 oz/315 g) all-purpose (plain) flour

2 eggs

3 tablespoons dry white wine

pinch of salt

SAUCE

11 oz (345 g) asparagus tips

3 tablespoons butter

shavings of Parmesan cheese (optional)

❖ For the filling, cook the asparagus in boiling salted water until bright green and tender; drain. Push the asparagus through a fine-mesh sieve into a mixing bowl. Add the ricotta, Parmesan, cream, and season to taste with salt and pepper. Mix well to combine.

❖ For the pasta, heap the flour on a work surface and make a well in the center. Add the eggs, wine, and salt and knead to a smooth, elastic dough.

❖ Roll out the dough into 2 thin sheets of equal size. Place the filling on 1 pasta sheet in ½-teaspoon amounts, 2 inches (5 cm) apart. Top with the second sheet and press down gently around each mound of filling. Use a 2-inch (5-cm) cookie cutter or glass to cut out tortellini. Roll each around the end of your index finger and press the ends together.

❖ For the sauce, cook the asparagus in boiling salted water until bright green and just tender. Reserve 12 tips for decoration and slice the remaining tips. Melt the butter in a frying pan over low heat. Add the sliced asparagus and cook, stirring, until it just softens.

❖ In a large saucepan of boiling salted water cook the tortellini until they rise to the surface; drain. Serve topped with the hot sauce and reserved asparagus tips. Sprinkle with a few shavings of Parmesan cheese, if desired.

bucatini
with ginger carrots

serves 4

1 lb (500 g) carrots, cut into julienne strips

½ cup (4 oz/125 g) butter

2 teaspoons brown sugar

2 teaspoons white wine vinegar

1 tablespoon cumin seeds

1 piece (½ inch/1 cm) ginger,
finely chopped

¼ cup (2 fl oz/60 ml) coconut milk

3 tablespoons finely chopped cilantro
(fresh coriander) leaves

8 oz (250 g) bucatini (hollow spaghetti)

toasted sesame seeds, for garnish

❖ Steam the carrots until they are just tender. Melt the butter in a frying pan and stir in the sugar and vinegar until the mixture is well combined. Add the cumin seeds and ginger and cook, stirring, for a few minutes. Stir in the coconut milk and heat through. Add the carrots and cilantro and stir until heated through.

❖ In a large saucepan of boiling salted water cook the pasta until al dente. Drain and stir into the carrot mixture. Serve immediately, garnished with sesame seeds.

tagliatelle
with asparagus

serves 4–6 as an appetizer

8 oz (250 g) fresh plain tagliatelle

8 oz (250 g) fresh spinach tagliatelle

2 tablespoons olive oil

2 medium onions, chopped

2 cloves garlic, crushed

6 green (spring) onions, chopped

½ cup (4 fl oz/125 ml) dry white wine

1¼ cups (10 fl oz/315 ml) heavy (double) cream

⅓ cup (2½ fl oz/80 ml) sour cream

⅓ cup (½ oz/10 g) shredded fresh basil

1 cup (4 oz/125 g) grated Parmesan cheese

1 large bunch asparagus, cut into short lengths

shavings of Parmesan cheese, to serve

❖ In a large saucepan of boiling salted water cook the pasta until al dente; drain.

❖ Meanwhile, heat the oil in a large frying pan. Add the onions and garlic and cook, stirring often, until the onions are soft. Add the green onions and stir until soft. Stir in the wine, cream, sour cream, basil, and grated cheese. Stir until heated through but do not allow to boil.

❖ Cook the asparagus in boiling water until bright green and just tender. Drain.

❖ Stir the sauce into the pasta and serve immediately, topped with the asparagus and Parmesan shavings.

fried ravioli

serves 4

FILLING

²/₃ cup (4 oz/125 g) fresh, or ¹/₃ cup
(2 oz/60 g) dried, cannellini beans

2 lb (1 kg) peeled pumpkin,
coarsely chopped

¹/₃ cup (2 oz/60 g) cooked long-grain rice

2 eggs, beaten

¹/₂ cup (2 oz/60 g) grated Parmesan cheese

¹/₄ cup (1 oz/30 g) grated pecorino
romano cheese

1 clove garlic

¹/₂ cup (³/₄ oz/20 g) chopped fresh
flat-leaf (Italian) parsley

¹/₂ cup (³/₄ oz/20 g) chopped fresh marjoram

salt and ground pepper

¹/₄ cup (2 fl oz/60 ml) extra virgin olive oil

PASTA

4 cups (1 lb/500 g) all-purpose (plain) flour

pinch of salt

water, as needed

olive oil, for deep-frying

❖ For the filling, if using fresh cannellini beans cook them in a large saucepan of boiling salted water for 35 minutes, or until they are tender. If using dried beans, soak them for 12 hours in cold water, then cook for 45 minutes, or until tender. Drain.

❖ Preheat an oven to 350°F (180°C/Gas Mark 4). Place the pumpkin on a baking sheet lined with parchment (baking) paper and bake for 30 minutes, or until tender. Allow to cool, then place in a mixing bowl with the beans and rice. Stir in the eggs, cheeses, garlic, and herbs. Season to taste with salt and pepper. Add the olive oil and mix until combined.

❖ For the pasta, place the flour and salt in a large mixing bowl and add just enough water to make a very soft dough. Set aside for 30 minutes, covered with a damp kitchen towel.

❖ Roll out the dough until it is $\frac{1}{16}$-inch (1-mm) thick and cut into 4-inch (10-cm) squares. Place 1 tablespoon of the filling in the center of each square. Fold the dough over diagonally to form large triangles and press the edges to secure.

❖ Fry the ravioli in very hot oil, using a slotted spoon to remove them when they are golden brown. Serve immediately.

summer
spaghetti

serves 4–6

1 lb (500 g) firm ripe tomatoes, peeled,
seeded, and finely chopped

1 red (Spanish) onion, diced

1 small fresh red chile, seeded
and finely chopped

12 stuffed green olives, finely chopped

1 tablespoon capers, roughly chopped

1½ teaspoons finely chopped fresh oregano

⅓ cup (⅓ oz/10 g) finely chopped fresh
flat-leaf (Italian) parsley

2 cloves garlic, crushed

½ cup (4 fl oz/125 ml) extra virgin olive oil

1 lb (500 g) spaghetti

❖ Combine all the ingredients, except the
pasta, in a large bowl. Mix well, cover, and
set aside overnight.

❖ In a large saucepan of boiling salted
water cook the pasta until al dente; drain.
Serve topped with the tomato mixture.

farfalle
with onion and herbs

serves 4–6

1½ tablespoons olive oil

1½ lb (750 g) white onions, thinly sliced

1 teaspoon honey

pinch of ground nutmeg

2 cloves garlic, crushed

3 cups (24 fl oz/750 ml) chicken
or vegetable stock

1 lb (500 g) farfalle (bow-tie pasta)

2 tablespoons grated Parmesan cheese

2 teaspoons chopped fresh marjoram

1 teaspoon chopped fresh thyme

1½ tablespoons chopped fresh parsley

1½ tablespoons sherry vinegar

❖ Heat the oil in a large saucepan over medium heat. Add the onions and toss to coat them in oil. Cover and cook over low heat, stirring occasionally, for 20 minutes. Add the honey, nutmeg, and garlic and cook, stirring often, for 5 minutes. Add the stock and simmer for about 15 minutes, or until the liquid reduces by half.

❖ Meanwhile, in a large saucepan of boiling salted water cook the pasta until al dente; drain well.

❖ Stir the cheese, herbs, and vinegar into the onion mixture. Add the pasta and stir until heated through. Serve immediately.

eggplant, tomato, and pasta gratin

3 medium eggplants (aubergines), about 3 lb (1.5 kg)
total weight

salt and ground pepper

2 tablespoons olive oil

2 onions, chopped

2 cloves garlic, chopped

1 can (14½ oz/455 g) plum (Roma) tomatoes

2 tablespoons tomato paste

2 teaspoons dried basil

1 teaspoon dried oregano

salt and pepper

olive oil, extra, for frying

8 oz (250 g) penne or other short pasta

10 oz (315 g) mozzarella cheese, sliced

❖ Grease an 8-cup (2-qt/2-l) gratin dish.

❖ Wash the eggplants and cut crosswise into thin slices. Place in a colander and sprinkle the cut surfaces with salt. Set aside for about 30 minutes to rid them of their bitter juices. Rinse the eggplant slices under cold running water, place on paper towels, and pat dry thoroughly.

❖ Heat the oil in a large saucepan. Add the onions and garlic and cook, stirring often, until the onions are soft. Stir in the undrained tomatoes, tomato paste, basil, and oregano. Bring to a boil, reduce heat, and simmer for 30 minutes, or until thickened. Season with salt and pepper.

❖ Meanwhile, in a large frying pan heat 2–3 tablespoons of the extra olive oil. Working in batches, fry the eggplant slices on both sides until golden and cooked through. Add more oil as necessary. Place the eggplant slices on paper towels to drain.

❖ Preheat an oven to 350°F (180°C/Gas Mark 4).

❖ In a large saucepan of boiling salted water cook the pasta until al dente. Drain well and stir into the tomato mixture. Layer a third of the eggplant slices in the gratin dish and top with half of the pasta mixture. Top with half of the remaining eggplant slices, half of the mozzarella, then the remaining pasta mixture. Finish with the remaining eggplant slices, then mozzarella.

❖ Bake, uncovered, for 30 minutes, or until the mozzarella is melted and golden.

spaghettini
with cilantro pesto

serves 4

1 lb (500 g) spaghettini

1 cup (3½ oz/100 g) hazelnuts (filberts), toasted, skins removed, roughly chopped

1 bunch (1⅔ oz/50 g) cilantro (fresh coriander) leaves

1 small clove garlic, chopped

1 teaspoon salt

2 tablespoons hazelnut oil (or olive oil)

3 tablespoons olive oil

1 tablespoon butter

4 oz (125 g) shaved Parmesan cheese (optional)

❖ In a large saucepan of boiling salted water cook the pasta until al dente.

❖ Meanwhile, place the hazelnuts, cilantro, garlic, and salt in a food processor and process until roughly chopped. While the motor is running, gradually add the hazelnut and olive oils. The mixture should be well chopped and mixed but not puréed.

❖ Drain the pasta and place in a large bowl. Add the butter and cheese and toss the pasta to combine. Add the pesto and toss until the pasta is thoroughly coated.

❖ Serve immediately, sprinkled with shavings of Parmesan cheese, if desired.

fusilli with pecans

serves 6 as an appetizer

1 lb (500 g) fusilli

3 tablespoons butter

1 clove garlic, finely chopped

5 oz (155 g) pecans, chopped

5 oz (155 g) cream cheese

½ cup (4 fl oz/125 ml) heavy
(double) cream

½ cup (2 oz/60 g) grated
Parmesan cheese

❖ In a large saucepan of boiling salted water cook the pasta until al dente; drain.

❖ Meanwhile, in a large frying pan melt the butter and gently fry the garlic until golden. Add the pecans and cook, stirring often, for 3 minutes. Remove from heat.

❖ Add the cream cheese to the frying pan and heat gently. Gradually stir in the cream and continue cooking gently until the mixture is warmed through.

❖ Add the Parmesan to the pasta and toss to combine. Add the sauce and toss until the pasta is thoroughly coated. Serve immediately.

ratatouille
lasagne

serves 4

2 medium eggplants (aubergines), sliced into rounds

4 zucchini (courgettes), cut into julienne strips

1/3 cup (2 1/2 fl oz/80 ml) olive oil

1 onion, diced

1 clove garlic, crushed

1 can (14 1/2 oz/455 g) peeled tomatoes

1 teaspoon tomato paste

salt and ground pepper

1 1/2 red bell peppers (capsicums)

BECHAMEL SAUCE

1 tablespoon butter

2 tablespoons all-purpose (plain) flour

1 cup (8 fl oz/250 ml) milk

1/2 cup (4 fl oz/125 ml) heavy (double) cream

1 lb (500 g) lasagne noodles

1 1/3 cups (5 oz/155 g) grated Parmesan cheese

4 bocconcini (fresh mozzarella) cheeses, sliced

❖ Place the eggplant slices in a colander, sprinkle with salt, and set aside for 30 minutes. Rinse and pat dry with paper towels. Preheat an oven to 325°F (160°C/Gas Mark 3). Blanch the zucchini in boiling water; drain.

❖ Meanwhile, heat 2 tablespoons of the olive oil in a saucepan. Add the onion and garlic and cook until soft. Add the undrained tomatoes, tomato paste, and salt and pepper to taste. Simmer, stirring occasionally, until thick. Set aside. Heat the remaining oil in a frying pan and fry the eggplant in batches until golden on both sides and just cooked through. Set aside.

❖ Cut the whole bell pepper in half. Remove seeds and membranes. Place bell pepper halves, skin-side up, under a hot broiler (griller) and cook until the skin blisters and blackens. Place in a sealed heavy-duty plastic bag and set aside until cool. Remove the skin and cut into thick strips.

❖ For the béchamel sauce, melt the butter in a saucepan. Stir in the flour and cook over low heat for 2 minutes. Remove from the heat and gradually stir in the milk and cream. Return to the heat and cook, stirring, until the mixture thickens. Thin with a little extra milk, if necessary.

❖ Cook the lasagne noodles according to the manufacturer's instructions; drain. Place 4 lasagne noodles in a large, lightly oiled baking dish. Spread a generous tablespoon of béchamel sauce over each. Top with the tomato mixture and sprinkle with some of the Parmesan. Continue layering as follows: pasta, béchamel sauce, zucchini, bell pepper, Parmesan, pasta, béchamel sauce, eggplant, bocconcini, pasta, béchamel sauce, Parmesan.

❖ Bake until the lasagne is cooked through and the cheeses have melted, 30–40 minutes.

tagliatelle
with egg and bread crumbs

In Italy, this dish was (and still is) often served in a freshly made puff or shortcrust pastry case, either open or closed according to the whim of the cook. Omitting the pastry makes the dish both simpler and lighter.

1 lb (500 g) spinach, washed and trimmed

2½ cups (10 oz/315 g) all-purpose (plain) flour

pinch of salt

3 eggs

⅓ cup (3 oz/90 g) butter

1 cup (4 oz/125 g) fine, dried bread crumbs

2 hard-boiled eggs, chopped

❖ Cook the spinach in a small amount of boiling water for a few minutes, until it wilts. Drain and squeeze out the excess liquid. Process spinach in a food processor until finely chopped.

❖ Sift the flour into a mound on a work surface. Make a well in the center and add the salt, eggs, and spinach. Knead the mixture into a soft, smooth dough. Lightly flour the work surface and roll out the dough until it is as thin as possible. Roll up the sheet of dough and slice into ¼-inch (5-mm) wide tagliatelle.

❖ In a wide, shallow saucepan of boiling salted water cook the tagliatelle until the strands begin to rise to the surface; drain well.

❖ Meanwhile, melt 3 tablespoons of the butter in a small saucepan. Add the bread crumbs and fry gently for a few minutes. Add the remaining butter and heat until it just melts. Add to the tagliatelle and toss to combine. Serve immediately, sprinkled with the hard-boiled egg.

fried gnocchi

serves 6

Serve the gnocchi accompanied by a simple green salad, lightly dressed with extra virgin olive oil and balsamic vinegar.

¼ oz (7 g) yeast

½ cup (4 fl oz/125 ml) milk, warmed to blood heat

1½ cups (6 oz/185 g) all-purpose (plain) flour

pinch of salt

7 oz (220 g) salami, thinly sliced

4 oz (125 g) Parmesan cheese, sliced

4 cups (32 fl oz/1 liter) olive oil

✤ Dissolve the yeast in the milk. Heap the flour on a work surface and make a well in the center. Add the yeast mixture and salt. Work the mixture into a soft dough. Shape into a ball and set aside in a warm place, covered, until the dough has doubled in volume. Roll out the dough into a rectangle, then fold the rectangle into quarters. Roll and fold the dough this way 4 more times. Finally, roll the dough into a thin sheet and cut into 2 x 4-inch (5 x 10-cm) rectangles.

✤ Place a slice of salami and a slice of cheese on half of each piece of dough. Fold each rectangle over to enclose the filling, moistening the edges a little to secure. Heat the oil until very hot and deep-fry the rectangles of dough, a few at a time, until they are puffed and browned. Transfer the gnocchi to paper towels to drain. Serve immediately.

recipe variations

This gnocchi can easily be varied by using different fillings. Try replacing the Parmesan cheese with Gouda, Gruyère, Cheddar or Fontina cheese. Or use prosciutto or ham instead of the salami.

rainbow lasagne

serves 6–8

This dish is named for the colorful layers of spinach, red bell pepper, tomatoes, corn and cheese sauce that look and taste wonderful.

5 tablespoons (2½ oz/75 g) butter

5 tablespoons (1½ oz/45 g) all-purpose (plain) flour

4 cups (32 fl oz/1 liter) milk

salt and ground white pepper

½ teaspoon sharp mustard

2 cups (8 oz/250 g) grated mozzarella cheese

1 lb (500 g) chopped frozen or fresh spinach

½ teaspoon grated nutmeg

3 tablespoons olive oil

2 medium onions, sliced

1 large red bell pepper (capsicum), seeded and sliced

2 cups (12 oz/375 g) corn kernels

1 lb (500 g) curly instant lasagne noodles or partially cooked dried lasagne noodles

3 large tomatoes, sliced

1½ cups (12 fl oz/375 ml) Herb and Tomato Sauce (page 101), or purchased Italian-style tomato sauce

❖ Preheat an oven to 350°F (180°C/Gas Mark 4).

❖ In a medium saucepan melt the butter and stir in the flour. Remove from the heat, add the milk, and stir until smooth. Return to medium heat and stir until the mixture thickens. Season to taste with salt and pepper and add the mustard. Stir in three-fourths of the cheese. Cover the surface with plastic wrap to prevent a skin forming and set aside.

❖ Place the spinach in a saucepan over low heat and cover briefly to make it sweat. Remove the lid and increase the heat to boil off the liquid. Season to taste with salt and pepper and add the nutmeg. Set aside. Heat 2 tablespoons of the oil in a frying pan and cook the onions until they soften and are lightly colored; set aside. Add the remaining oil and cook the bell pepper until it softens; set aside. Cook the corn in lightly salted water until just tender; drain.

❖ Add half of the onion and a third of the cheese sauce to the spinach; stir to combine. Add the corn and half of the remaining cheese sauce to the remaining onion; stir to combine.

❖ Place a layer of lasagne noodles in a lightly greased baking dish. Top with the spinach mixture. Cover with another layer of pasta, then the bell pepper and sliced tomatoes. Pour the tomato sauce over the top. Cover with another layer of pasta, then the corn mixture. Top with a final layer of pasta and spread with the remaining cheese sauce. Sprinkle with the remaining cheese. Bake for about 45 minutes, or until cooked through.

serves 2

9 oz (280 g) purchased
ravioli, or homemade
Mushroom-Filled Ravioli
(pages 124–125) or
Meat-Stuffed Ravioli
(pages 220–221)

3 tablespoons butter
or margarine

1 oz (30 g) chopped walnuts,
pecans, or almonds

4 green (spring) onions,
thinly sliced

1 teaspoon peeled and
grated fresh ginger

1½ oz (45 g) crumbled feta
cheese or blue cheese,
or grated Parmesan
cheese (optional)

❖ In a large saucepan of boiling salted water cook the pasta until al dente, 6–8 minutes. (Or, cook according to package directions.) Drain.

❖ Meanwhile, melt the butter or margarine in a medium frying pan. Add the nuts, green onions, and ginger and cook, stirring, for 3–4 minutes, or until the nuts are lightly toasted and the onions are tender. Add to the hot cooked ravioli; mix well.

❖ Serve immediately, sprinkled with blue cheese, feta cheese, or Parmesan cheese, if desired.

nutty ravioli

eggplant
charleston

serves 4

4 medium-large
eggplants (aubergines)

vegetable oil, for
deep-frying

5 cups (40 fl oz/1.25 l)
tomato purée

1 cup (1 oz/30 g) fresh
basil leaves, chopped

1¼ lb (625 g) fresh small
gnocchi or pasta shells, or
¾ lb (375 g) dried pasta

5 oz (155 g) mozzarella
cheese, diced

1 cup (4 oz/125 g) grated
Parmesan cheese

salt and ground pepper

❖ Cut a slice from the side of each eggplant; scoop out the pulp and cut it into small dice. Deep-fry the eggplant cases, one at a time, in hot oil until golden (the cases must be covered in oil). Drain on paper towels and set aside. Deep-fry the diced pulp until golden. Drain on paper towels.

❖ In a frying pan, combine the tomato purée, basil, and fried eggplant pulp. Cook until the mixture is heated through.

❖ Meanwhile, in a large saucepan of boiling salted water cook the gnocchi or pasta until al dente; drain. Add to the sauce and stir in the cheeses. Season to taste with salt and pepper, spoon into the eggplant cases, and serve immediately.

gnocchi with pesto

serves 4

PESTO

1 large bunch fresh basil

1–2 cloves garlic,
roughly chopped

1 cup (4 oz/125 g) grated
Parmesan cheese, plus extra
for sprinkling

2 tablespoons pine nuts

1 teaspoon salt

½ cup (4 fl oz/125 ml) extra
virgin olive oil

1 lb (500 g) purchased
fresh gnocchi

2 tablespoons
toasted pine nuts (optional)

❖ Wash the basil. Pick off and reserve the leaves; discard stems.

❖ Place the basil, garlic, cheese, pine nuts, and salt in a food processor. Process until the ingredients are chopped. While the motor is running, gradually add the olive oil and process until the ingredients are finely chopped and the mixture is smooth.

❖ In a large saucepan bring plenty of salted water to a boil. Add the gnocchi to the boiling water and cook until they rise to the surface, about 5 minutes. Drain and place in a warmed serving bowl. Add the pesto and mix carefully until well combined. Serve sprinkled with extra Parmesan and pine nuts, if desired.

tricolor pasta
with summer vegetables

serves 4–6

*4 oz (125 g) tomato-flavored dried
tagliatelle or fettuccine*

*4 oz (125 g) spinach-flavored dried
tagliatelle or fettuccine*

4 oz (125 g) plain dried tagliatelle or fettuccine

½ cup (3 oz/90 g) fresh or thawed frozen green peas

4 spears fresh asparagus

1 medium zucchini (courgette), sliced

12 cherry tomatoes

12 large snow peas (mangetouts), trimmed

1 green (spring) onion, finely shredded

1½ tablespoons olive oil

1½ tablespoons butter

¼ cup (1 oz/30 g) finely grated Parmesan cheese

ground black pepper

1½ teaspoons finely chopped fresh basil

❖ In a large saucepan of boiling salted water cook the pasta until al dente. Drain.

❖ Meanwhile, in a small saucepan simmer the peas in lightly salted water for about 4 minutes; remove with a slotted spoon and set aside. Cut the asparagus into ¾-inch (2-cm) lengths and add to the saucepan with the zucchini and the cherry tomatoes. Cook for 3 minutes, then remove with a slotted spoon. Cut the cherry tomatoes in half. Add the asparagus, zucchini, and tomatoes to the peas. Add the snow peas to the saucepan and cook for 30 seconds. Remove, cut into shreds, and add to the other vegetables.

❖ Toss the pasta with the cooked vegetables, the green onion, olive oil, butter, and half of the cheese. Serve sprinkled with pepper, the remaining cheese, and the basil.

rigatoni
with roasted vegetable
sauce

serves 4–6

4 ripe tomatoes

1 large red bell pepper (capsicum), quartered, seeds removed

1 small head garlic, excess papery skin removed

1 tablespoon olive oil

1 tablespoon balsamic vinegar

salt and ground black pepper

8 oz (500 g) rigatoni

3½ oz (105 g) drained oil-packed sun-dried tomatoes, roughly chopped

3½ oz (105 g) small black olives

❖ Preheat an oven to 350°F (180°C/Gas Mark 4). Place the tomatoes, bell pepper, and garlic in a baking pan. Brush with the oil and bake for 30 minutes.

❖ Set the vegetables aside to cool slightly. Squeeze the garlic out of its shells and peel the tomatoes and bell pepper. Place in a food processor with the vinegar and process until the mixture is almost smooth but still has some texture. Season to taste with salt and pepper.

❖ In a large saucepan of boiling salted water cook the pasta until al dente; drain.

❖ Meanwhile, heat the sauce in a saucepan. Add the sun-dried tomatoes and olives and cook until heated through. Add the pasta to the sauce and mix well. Serve immediately.

lemon and parsley
tagliatelle

serves 4

8 oz (250 g) dried or 1 lb (500 g) fresh tagliatelle

2 tablespoons olive oil

¼ cup (2 oz/60 g) butter

2 small onions, chopped

1 tablespoon grated lemon zest (rind)

½ cup (3 oz/90 g) pitted, chopped green olives

½ cup (¾ oz/20 g) chopped fresh flat-leaf
(Italian) parsley

❖ In a large saucepan of boiling salted water cook the pasta until al dente; drain. Return to the pan and add the oil, butter, onions, lemon zest, olives, and parsley. Mix well and heat through. Serve immediately.

polenta gnocchi
with sage and butter

serves 6

6 cups (48 fl oz/1.5 l) water

salt

3¼ cups (13 oz/400 g) yellow cornmeal (polenta)

⅓ cup (3 oz/90 g) butter

handful of fresh sage leaves

❖ Add the water to a large saucepan, salt it lightly, and bring to a boil. Add the cornmeal, stirring constantly with a wooden spoon. Cook for about 30 minutes, or until the mixture comes away from the side of the pan.

❖ Preheat an oven to 400°F (200°C/Gas Mark 5). Use 2 tablespoons of the butter to coat a baking dish. Shape the polenta into large oval shapes using a tablespoon dipped in cold water. Place the polenta gnocchi in the prepared baking dish.

❖ In a small saucepan fry the sage in the remaining butter. Pour over the gnocchi and bake for 20 minutes. Serve immediately.

potato gnocchi
with tomato sauce

serves 4–6

This simple, uncooked tomato sauce makes a great topping for any kind of pasta. Add some thinly sliced green (spring) onion and finely chopped fresh chile for a spicier flavor.

TOMATO SAUCE

8 medium tomatoes, peeled, seeded, and chopped

4 cloves garlic, finely chopped

¾ cup (¾ oz/20 g) loosely packed fresh basil leaves, torn

½ cup (4 fl oz/125 ml) olive oil

salt and ground pepper

GNOCCHI

1 lb (500 g) potatoes

1¾ cups (7 oz/220 g) all-purpose (plain) flour

½ teaspoon salt

1 teaspoon ground nutmeg

2–3 tablespoons butter, melted

❖ For the tomato sauce, place the tomatoes, garlic, and basil in a bowl. Stir in the olive oil, cover, and refrigerate for 2 hours.

❖ Steam the potatoes whole until cooked but firm; peel and set aside to cool. Heap the flour on a work surface and sprinkle with the salt and nutmeg. Mash the cooled potatoes (do not add butter or milk). Place the potato in the center of the flour and begin incorporating the flour with your hands, little by little, until all but ½ cup (2 oz/60 g) of the flour is incorporated. Begin to knead the potato mixture, incorporating the remaining flour. Knead for 5 minutes. Divide the mixture into 3 portions. Roll each portion into a roll, ½ inch (1 cm) in diameter. Cut each roll into 1-inch (2.5-cm) pieces of gnocchi and press each piece against the tines of a fork.

❖ Bring a large saucepan of salted water to the boil. Add the gnocchi, one at a time and gently stir with a wooden spoon. Cook until the gnocchi rise to the surface, then cook for 1 minute more. Place the melted butter in a large warmed serving dish. Use a slotted spoon to transfer the gnocchi, as they are cooked, to the dish.

❖ Season the tomato sauce with salt and pepper. Add to the gnocchi and mix until combined.

macaroni gratin with mushrooms

serves 4–6

In this recipe, wild mushrooms are prepared simply with pasta, shallots, and herbs. If fresh wild mushrooms prove hard to find, substitute 9 oz (280 g) assorted dried ones. To reconstitute them, soak in cold water for a few hours, then drain and squeeze out any excess liquid.

1½ cups (5 oz/155 g) elbow macaroni

2 tablespoons olive oil

2 tablespoons chopped shallots

5 oz (155 g) fresh chanterelle mushrooms, brushed clean, stems trimmed

4 oz (125 g) fresh shiitake mushrooms, brushed clean, stems trimmed

2 oz (60 g) fresh oyster mushrooms, brushed clean, stems trimmed

salt and ground pepper

1 tablespoon chopped fresh chives

1 tablespoon chopped fresh parsley

2 cups (8 oz/250 g) finely shredded Swiss cheese

❖ In a large saucepan of boiling salted water cook the pasta until al dente, about 5 minutes.

❖ Meanwhile, heat the olive oil in a large saucepan over medium-low heat. Add the shallots and cook, stirring, until translucent, about 2 minutes.

❖ Cut any large mushrooms in half. Add all of the mushrooms and salt and pepper, to taste, to the shallots and cook over medium heat, stirring often, until the mushrooms are soft and slightly browned, 4–5 minutes.

❖ Drain the pasta and add to the mushroom mixture. Stir in the chives and parsley. Taste and adjust the seasoning, if necessary.

❖ Transfer the mixture to a flameproof 9-inch (23-cm) gratin dish with 2-inch (5-cm) high sides or individual gratin dishes. Sprinkle evenly with the cheese. Place under a hot broiler (griller) until the cheese melts, about 2 minutes. Serve immediately.

macaroni
and cheese

serves 3–4

2½ cups (9 oz/280 g) elbow macaroni

1 tablespoon vegetable oil or olive oil

SAUCE

3 tablespoons butter

3 tablespoons all-purpose (plain) flour

2½ cups (20 fl oz/625 ml) milk, warmed

1¾ cups (7 oz/220 g) shredded
sharp Cheddar cheese

½ teaspoon salt

½ teaspoon ground pepper

2 teaspoons Dijon mustard

1 teaspoon finely chopped fresh parsley

TOPPING

¾ cup (3 oz/90 g) shredded
sharp Cheddar cheese

½ cup (1 oz/30 g) fresh bread crumbs

1 teaspoon butter, cut into small pieces

❖ Preheat an oven to 375°F (190°C/Gas Mark 4). Lightly butter an 8-inch (20-cm) square baking pan or dish.

❖ In a large saucepan of boiling salted water cook the pasta until al dente, 5–7 minutes, or according to package directions. Drain and rinse under cold running water to remove any excess starch. Place in a large mixing bowl and drizzle with the oil. Set aside.

❖ For the sauce, melt the butter in a saucepan over medium-low heat. Sprinkle with the flour and whisk until the flour is absorbed and the mixture is gently bubbling and lightly golden, 2–3 minutes. Gradually add the warmed milk, whisking constantly, and bring to a simmer. Continue to simmer, whisking constantly, until smooth and slightly thickened, 3–4 minutes.

❖ Add the cheese to the sauce, remove from the heat, and whisk constantly until the cheese melts. Stir in the salt, pepper, mustard, and parsley. Pour the sauce over the pasta and mix to combine. Transfer the pasta mixture to the prepared baking pan.

❖ For the topping, in a small bowl combine the cheese and bread crumbs. Sprinkle evenly over the pasta mixture. Dot with the butter.

❖ Bake until the topping bubbles and begins to form a crust, 20–25 minutes (cover the surface with aluminum foil if it begins to brown too much). Remove from the oven and set aside for about 5 minutes before serving.

summer linguine

serves 4–6

¼ cup (2 fl oz/60 ml) extra virgin olive oil

1 shallot, finely chopped

2 cloves garlic, finely chopped

2 russet or golden-fleshed potatoes, peeled and cut into small dice

1 zucchini (courgette), trimmed, halved lengthwise, then sliced into half-moons

8 oz (250 g) green beans, ends trimmed

8 oz (250 g) zucchini (courgette) flowers, stamens removed (optional)

¼ cup (⅓ oz/10 g) coarsely chopped fresh basil

salt and ground pepper

juice of ½ lemon, or to taste

1 lb (500 g) linguine

2 tablespoons sweet (unsalted) butter, at room temperature

grated Parmesan cheese, to serve

❖ Heat the olive oil in a frying pan over medium-low heat. Add the shallot and garlic and cook, stirring often, just until the flavors are released, a few seconds. Add the potatoes and cook, gently tossing once or twice, until just tender, about 7 minutes. Add the zucchini, green beans, zucchini flowers (if using), and basil. Cook, stirring occasionally, until all the vegetables are tender, about 10 minutes. Season with salt, pepper, and lemon juice to taste.

❖ Meanwhile, in a large saucepan of boiling salted water cook the pasta until al dente. Reserve ½ cup (4 fl oz/125 ml) of the cooking water. Drain the pasta.

❖ Place the vegetable mixture and reserved cooking water in a large serving bowl. Add the pasta and butter and toss to combine. Serve immediately accompanied by the cheese.

orecchiette

with tomato-shallot sauce

serves 4–6

Roman cooks are famous for hot pasta tossed in a mixture of chopped tomatoes, garlic, basil, and oil. Variations on this easy, tasty, and colorful dish are now found all over Italy. Since the ingredients are already on hand when making pizzas, this dish can often be found on many pizzeria menus, especially on warm summer nights.

10 firm, ripe plum (Roma) tomatoes, chopped

2 shallots, finely chopped

2 cloves garlic, finely chopped

1–2 tablespoons capers, rinsed, drained, and coarsely chopped

¼ cup (2 fl oz/60 ml) balsamic vinegar

½–1 cup (4–8 fl oz/125–250 ml) extra virgin olive oil

small handful of coarsely chopped fresh flat-leaf (Italian) parsley

10 fresh basil leaves, chopped

salt and ground pepper

1 lb (500 g) orecchiette

In a large, shallow bowl combine the tomatoes, shallots, garlic, capers, vinegar, ½ cup (4 fl oz/125 ml) of the olive oil, the parsley, basil, and salt and pepper to taste. If a fuller, richer flavor is desired, add all or part of the remaining ½ cup (4 fl oz/125 ml) olive oil. Toss well, cover, and set aside in a cool place for 1–3 hours.

When you are ready to serve the meal, cook the pasta in a large saucepan of salted boiling water until al dente. Drain well and add to the tomato mixture. Toss to combine, and serve immediately.

food fact

Capers are the unopened buds of a bush native to the Mediterranean, and are sold pickled in brine, vinegar, or wine. Smaller capers have a more delicate flavor and are more aromatic. The sourish, somewhat bitter flavor of capers adds a piquant note to savory dishes. Capers must be kept covered with a liquid, or they develop an unpleasant taste. Always rinse them before using.

lasagna
with four cheeses

serves 6–8

BECHAMEL SAUCE

3¹/₂ cups (28 fl oz/875 ml) milk

1 fresh rosemary sprig, 2 inches (5 cm) long

¹/₃ cup (3 oz/90 g) sweet (unsalted) butter

5 tablespoons (1¹/₂ oz/45 g) all-purpose (plain) flour

salt and ground pepper

GARLIC BREAD CRUMBS

1 loaf coarse country bread, about 8 oz (250 g), cut into 1-inch (2.5-cm) cubes

1 tablespoon finely chopped garlic, or to taste

salt and ground pepper

extra virgin olive oil, as needed

CHEESE FILLING

¹/₂ cup (2 oz/60 g) walnuts

1¹/₂ cups (12 oz/375 g) ricotta cheese

³/₄ cup (6 oz/185 g) mascarpone cheese

³/₄ cup (3 oz/90 g) shredded fontina cheese

2 cups (8 oz/250 g) grated Parmesan cheese

1 tablespoon finely chopped fresh rosemary

3 tablespoons chopped fresh flat-leaf (Italian) parsley

salt and ground pepper

20 sheets "no-boil" lasagna

❖ For the béchamel sauce, pour the milk into a saucepan, add the rosemary sprig, and warm over medium-low heat until small bubbles appear around the sides of the pan. Melt the butter in a separate saucepan over medium-low heat. Add the flour and whisk to form a smooth paste. Reduce heat to low and cook, stirring, for 2 minutes. When the milk is hot, gradually add to the flour mixture, whisking constantly. Simmer over medium heat until the sauce thickens enough to coat the back of a spoon, about 20 minutes. Remove and discard the rosemary sprig. Season to taste with salt and pepper. Cover the surface with plastic wrap and set aside to cool.

❖ For the garlic bread crumbs, preheat an oven to 350°F (180°C/Gas Mark 4). In a food processor, pulse the bread cubes to produce coarse crumbs. In a large bowl combine the bread crumbs, garlic, and salt and pepper to taste. Add just enough olive oil to moisten the mixture slightly. Spread the bread mixture over a baking sheet and bake until lightly golden, 2–4 minutes. Set aside.

❖ For the cheese filling, spread the walnuts over a baking sheet and toast until golden and fragrant, about 10 minutes. Set aside to cool. Increase oven temperature to 375°F (190°C/Gas Mark 4). In a large bowl combine the toasted walnuts, ricotta, mascarpone, fontina, 1 cup (4 oz/125 g) of the Parmesan, the rosemary, parsley, and salt and pepper to taste. Mix well. Add 1 cup (8 fl oz/250 ml) of the béchamel sauce and stir vigorously to combine.

❖ Bring a large saucepan of salted water to the boil. Using tongs, dip the "no-boil" lasagna sheets in the boiling water for 10 seconds, then lay them on a kitchen towel to drain.

lasagna with four cheeses

✤ Spread a thin layer of béchamel sauce over the base of a 13- x 9- x 2-inch (33- x 23- x 5-cm) baking dish. Top with a layer of pasta, then a layer of the cheese filling. Spread with another layer, ¼ inch (6 mm) thick, of béchamel sauce, then sprinkle with 1 tablespoon of the remaining Parmesan. Top with another layer of pasta. Alternate layers of the cheese mixture, béchamel sauce, Parmesan, and pasta, until all of the ingredients, except the Parmesan, are used up, ending with béchamel sauce. Sprinkle with the remaining Parmesan and the garlic bread crumbs.

✤ Cover with aluminum foil and bake until the top is bubbling, 35–40 minutes. Uncover and bake until the bread crumbs are crunchy, about 10 minutes longer. Set aside for 5–10 minutes before serving.

recipe variations

Try substituting pine nuts or almonds for the walnuts. The fontina cheese may be replaced with Cheddar, Gouda, or Monterey Jack.

spicy
tomato
sauce

makes 2 cups (16 fl oz/500 ml)

2 tablespoons olive oil

1 can (13½ oz/425 g) peeled tomatoes, chopped

1 clove garlic, finely chopped

1 small fresh red chile, chopped

4 anchovies in oil, drained, finely chopped

2 tablespoons finely chopped fresh flat-leaf
(Italian) parsley

1 tablespoon finely chopped fresh oregano

salt and ground black pepper

❖ Combine all the ingredients, except the salt and pepper, in a saucepan. Bring the mixture to a boil, then reduce the heat and simmer for 15 minutes or until the sauce has reduced and thickened. Season to taste with salt and pepper.

spinach–ricotta
dumplings

serves 4–6

BELL PEPPER SAUCE

4 large red bell peppers (capsicums)

2 tablespoons butter

2 tablespoons extra virgin olive oil

½ small yellow onion, finely diced

2 cloves garlic

1 cup (8 fl oz/250 ml) water
(or chicken or vegetable stock)

¼ cup (⅓ oz/10 g) coarsely chopped
fresh flat-leaf (Italian) parsley

5 fresh basil leaves

salt and ground pepper

2 tablespoons heavy (double)
cream (optional)

3 bunches spinach, about 1 lb (500 g) each,
stems removed

3 eggs, lightly beaten

¾ cup (3 oz/90 g) grated Parmesan cheese,
plus extra for garnish

¾ cup (3 oz/90 g) grated pecorino
romano cheese

2 cups (1 lb/500 g) ricotta cheese

3 tablespoons unbleached all-purpose
(plain) flour, plus extra for coating

salt and ground pepper

2 tablespoons butter, melted

½ cup (4 oz/125 g) butter, extra

10 fresh sage leaves

❖ For the bell pepper sauce, cut each bell pepper in half lengthwise and discard the stem, seeds, and membranes. Cut the bell peppers lengthwise into strips.

❖ Heat the butter and olive oil in a saucepan over medium heat. Add the onion and cook, stirring occasionally, until golden, about 7 minutes. Add the garlic and bell peppers and cook, stirring occasionally, until the bell peppers soften, about 10 minutes. Add the water or stock, parsley, and basil and bring to a simmer. Simmer, uncovered, until the bell peppers are tender, about 10 minutes. Season to taste with salt and pepper. Transfer to a food processor or blender and process or blend until smooth. Transfer to a bowl and stir in the cream, if using.

❖ Rinse the spinach but do not dry. Place in a large saucepan over medium-low heat, cover, and cook, tossing occasionally, until wilted, 2–4 minutes. Drain, squeeze to remove the excess liquid, and chop finely. In a bowl combine the spinach, eggs, Parmesan, pecorino romano, ricotta, flour, salt, and pepper. Stir until the mixture resembles a thick, slightly stiff batter. Add extra flour to a shallow dish to a depth of about ½ inch (13 mm). Shape the ricotta mixture into balls about ¾ inch (2 cm) in diameter. Roll the balls lightly in the flour to coat and then place them on a lightly floured tray.

❖ Preheat an oven to 250°F (120°C/Gas Mark 1). Bring a large saucepan of salted water to a gentle simmer. Add a few dumplings and cook, turning them occasionally to ensure they cook

spinach-ricotta dumplings

evenly, until they rise to the surface, and then cook for another minute or so; this should take about 3 minutes in all. Use a slotted spoon to transfer the dumplings to paper towels to drain. Place in an ovenproof dish, drizzle with the 2 tablespoons melted butter, and cover to keep warm. Repeat with the remaining dumplings.

❖ Meanwhile, in a saucepan over medium heat warm the bell pepper sauce. Melt the extra butter in a small saucepan over high heat. Add the sage leaves and cook, stirring often, until the sage leaves are crisp, about 5 minutes. Transfer to paper towels to drain.

❖ Pour the bell pepper sauce onto serving plates and place the dumplings on top. Top with the sage leaves and some of the butter they were cooked in. Serve immediately, garnished with extra Parmesan cheese.

linguine
with fava beans

serves 4–6

2 tablespoons extra
virgin olive oil

½ small onion, sliced

13 oz (410 g) shelled
fava (broad) beans

½ cup (4 fl oz/125 ml)
chicken stock

¼ cup (2 oz/60 g) butter

salt and ground pepper

13 oz (410 g) linguine

1 cup (4 oz/125 g) grated
Parmesan cheese

❖ Heat the oil in a saucepan over low heat. Add the onion and cook, stirring often, until it is translucent. Add the beans and stock and cook, stirring occasionally, for 20 minutes, or until the beans are tender. Add the butter, and salt and pepper to taste.

❖ In a large saucepan of boiling salted water cook the pasta until almost al dente. Drain. Add the pasta to the bean mixture and cook for a few minutes, stirring occasionally. Serve immediately, sprinkled with cheese.

orecchiette
with broccoli rabe, garlic, and pine nuts

serves 4

1 lb (500 g) broccoli rabe
(or regular broccoli)

12 oz (375 g) orecchiette

1 tablespoon butter

2 tablespoons extra virgin olive oil

½ cup (2½ oz/75 g) finely chopped
yellow onion

½ cup (2½ oz/75 g) pine nuts

1–2 small fresh red chiles, seeded and sliced

4 teaspoons finely chopped garlic

1½ cups (12 fl oz/375 ml)
vegetable or meat stock

2 tablespoons chopped fresh parsley

1 cup (1 oz/30 g) cilantro (fresh coriander)
leaves (optional)

salt and ground pepper

grated Parmesan or pecorino romano
cheese, for garnish

✧ Trim any tough portions from the broccoli rabe, then cut the stems and leaves into 1-inch (2.5-cm) lengths; leave the florets whole. Place the stems on a steamer rack over gently boiling water; cover and steam for 2–3 minutes. Add the leaves and florets and steam until cooked through but firm when pierced with a fork, 2–3 minutes longer. Set aside.

✧ In a large saucepan of boiling salted water cook the pasta until al dente.

✧ Meanwhile, heat the butter and olive oil in a large frying pan over medium heat. Add the onion and pine nuts and cook, stirring often, until the onion is translucent and the pine nuts are lightly golden, about 3 minutes. Add the chiles and garlic and cook, stirring, until very fragrant, a few seconds. Stir in the broccoli rabe and cook for 2 minutes. Stir in the stock and bring the mixture to a boil, then reduce heat to low and simmer for 1 minute.

✧ Drain the pasta and add to the frying pan. Toss to combine. Add the parsley and cilantro (if using) and toss to combine. Season to taste with salt and pepper. Serve immediately, sprinkled with cheese.

penne
with arugula

serves 4

Combining tomato sauce
with cream produces a
delicate, rose-colored sauce
whose mild, sweet flavor
complements the slight
saltiness of prosciutto and
pleasant pepperiness of
arugula. Other tubular pasta,
such as rigatoni, can be used
instead of the penne.

3 oz (90 g) prosciutto, finely diced

1¾ cups (14 fl oz/430 ml) Herb and Tomato Sauce
(page 101) or purchased bottled Italian-style
tomato sauce

1 cup (8 fl oz/250 ml) heavy (double) cream

3 oz (90 g) arugula (rocket), stems removed, chopped

salt and ground white pepper

1 lb (500 g) penne

❖ In a saucepan over medium heat combine the prosciutto with the tomato sauce. Bring to a simmer and simmer for 3–4 minutes. Stir in the cream and simmer for 1 minute more. Add the arugula and cook until it just wilts. Season to taste with salt and pepper.

❖ Meanwhile, in a large saucepan of boiling salted water cook the pasta until al dente. Drain the pasta and add to the sauce, stirring until the pasta is well coated. Serve immediately.

recipe variations

Bacon, ham, pancetta, or salami can be substituted for the prosciutto, if desired.

eggplant and walnut ravioli with pesto

**serves 8 as an appetizer
or 4 as a main course**

**Combine Genoa's signature pesto
sauce with tomato sauce and you
create *pesto corto*, which tops these
eggplant-filled ravioli and is also
delicious served with pasta ribbons.**

FILLING

*1 large eggplant (aubergine), peeled and
cut into rounds about ½ inch (13 mm) thick*

¼ cup (1 oz/30 g) walnuts, finely chopped

1 cup (8 oz/250 g) ricotta cheese

¼ cup (1 oz/30 g) grated Parmesan cheese

4 teaspoons finely chopped fresh parsley

2 tablespoons finely chopped fresh basil

1 tablespoon finely chopped fresh sage

salt and ground white pepper

12 oz (375 g) purchased thin
fresh pasta sheets

TOMATO–PESTO SAUCE

1/2 cup (1/2 oz/15 g) firmly packed
fresh basil leaves

1 1/2 teaspoons pine nuts

1 teaspoon finely chopped walnuts

1 clove garlic

3 tablespoons grated Parmesan cheese

1/3 cup (2 1/2 fl oz/80 ml) extra virgin olive oil

salt and ground white pepper

1 tablespoon butter

3/4 cup (6 fl oz/185 ml) Herb and
Tomato Sauce (page 101) or purchased
bottled Italian-style tomato sauce

2 oz (60 g) Parmesan cheese shavings

❖ For the filling, place the eggplant rounds
on a rack in a broiler pan and broil (grill)
until lightly browned, 3–4 minutes. Turn
the slices and broil (grill) until lightly
browned and tender, 2–3 minutes.

❖ Cut the eggplant into small pieces; you
should have about 1 cup (8 oz/250 g). Place
on paper towels to drain and allow to cool.

❖ Place the eggplant, walnuts, and 1/4 cup
(2 oz/60 g) of ricotta in a food processor
or blender. Process or blend until smooth.
Transfer to a bowl and stir in the remaining
ricotta, Parmesan, parsley, basil, and sage.
Cover and refrigerate for a few hours or
up to 1 day before using. Just before using,
season to taste with salt and white pepper.

❖ Using a cookie cutter 2 1/2 inches (6 cm)
in diameter, cut out 64 circles from the
pasta sheets. Cover the pasta circles with

eggplant and walnut ravioli with pesto

a damp kitchen towel to prevent them drying out; keep any remaining pasta for another use. Place 1 teaspoon of filling in the center of a pasta circle, brush the edges with a little water, and top with a second pasta circle. Gently press the edges to seal. Repeat with the remaining pasta circles and filling. Place in a single layer on a wire rack until slightly dry, 1–2 hours.

❖ Meanwhile, make the pesto for the sauce. Place the basil, pine nuts, walnuts, and garlic in a food processor and process until smooth. Add the cheese and process until combined. With the motor running, gradually add the oil in a steady stream. Season to taste with salt and pepper.

❖ In a large saucepan of boiling salted water cook the ravioli until al dente, 3–4 minutes.

❖ Meanwhile, melt the butter in a large frying pan over medium heat and stir in the tomato sauce. When the sauce is warm, add the pesto and stir to combine.

❖ Drain the ravioli and add to the tomato-pesto sauce. Stir gently to coat. Serve the ravioli and sauce immediately, sprinkled with Parmesan shavings.

sicilian gnocchi

serves 12

⅓ cup (2 oz/60 g) golden raisins (sultanas)

2 lb (1 kg) ricotta cheese

8 egg yolks

1½ oz (45 g) pine nuts, chopped

1¾ cups (7 oz/220 g) grated Parmesan cheese

3 tablespoons finely chopped fresh parsley

handful of finely chopped fresh basil

salt and ground black pepper

1½ cups (6 oz/180 g) all-purpose (plain) flour

¾ cup (6 oz/185 g) butter, melted

❖ Soak the raisins in a small bowl of water for about 30 minutes. Drain and pat dry.

❖ Push the ricotta through a fine-mesh sieve into a bowl. Add the raisins, egg yolks, pine nuts, half of the Parmesan, the parsley, and basil. Season with salt and pepper and mix well. Add 2 tablespoons of the flour and mix until combined. Use a teaspoon to shape the mixture into oval gnocchi, about the size of a small egg. Roll the gnocchi in the remaining flour.

❖ In a large saucepan of boiling salted water cook the gnocchi until they rise to the surface. Use a slotted spoon to transfer the gnocchi to a bowl. Add the melted butter and toss to combine. Serve immediately, sprinkled with the remaining Parmesan.

genoa pansotti
with artichokes

**serves 6 as an appetizer,
or 4 as a main course**

Along the Ligurian coast, on
the Gulf of Genoa in Italy,
herbs grow in profusion.
They add their distinctive
fragrance to a wealth of
local dishes, including these
pansotti cloaked with a
herb-laced butter sauce.

FILLING

*2 oz (60 g) steamed fresh (or thawed, frozen)
artichoke hearts*

¼ cup (2 oz/60 g) ricotta cheese

2 tablespoons mascarpone cheese

½ cup (2 oz/60 g) grated Parmesan cheese

1 teaspoon finely chopped arugula (rocket)

1 teaspoon finely chopped fresh parsley

¼ teaspoon finely chopped garlic

salt and ground white pepper

pinch of grated nutmeg

8 oz (250 g) purchased thin
fresh pasta sheets

SAUCE

1/4 cup (2 oz/60 g) sweet (unsalted) butter

1/2 cup (2 1/2 oz/75 g) chopped steamed fresh
(or thawed, frozen) artichoke hearts

2 tablespoons chopped fresh parsley,
basil, thyme, marjoram, sage, or chives,
or a mixture of herbs

1/4 cup (1/2 oz/15 g) thinly sliced
arugula (rocket)

salt and ground white pepper

❖ For the filling, place the artichokes and
ricotta in a blender or food processor and
blend or process until smooth. Place the
artichoke mixture, mascarpone, Parmesan,
arugula, parsley, and garlic in a bowl and
stir until very smooth. Cover and refrigerate
for 2 hours or up to 1 day. Just before
using, season to taste with salt and white
pepper, and add the nutmeg.

❖ Use a sharp knife to cut the pasta into
2-inch (5-cm) squares; you will need 48.
Cover the pasta squares with a damp
kitchen towel to prevent them drying out;
keep any remaining pasta for another use.

❖ Place about 1/2 teaspoon of filling in the
center of each pasta square. Brush the
edges of the squares with a little water and
fold each square in half to form a triangle.
Stretch the pasta, if necessary, so the points

genoa pansotti with artichokes

of the triangle meet. Gently press the edges together to seal. Place in a single layer on a wire rack until slightly dry to the touch, 1–2 hours.

❖ In a large saucepan of boiling salted water cook the pansotti until al dente, 2–3 minutes.

❖ Meanwhile, for the sauce, melt the butter in a large frying pan over low heat. Add the chopped artichokes and cook, stirring, until heated through, about 1 minute. Drain the pansotti and add to the artichokes. Increase heat to high and toss the pasta gently. Add the herbs and arugula and toss until combined. Season to taste with salt and pepper. Serve immediately.

herb and tomato sauce

**makes about 4 cups
(32 fl oz/1 liter)**

*4 lb (2 kg) ripe plum (Roma)
tomatoes or 45 oz (1.4 kg)
canned peeled tomatoes*

2 tablespoons olive oil

2 cloves garlic, finely chopped

½ teaspoon salt

½ teaspoon sugar

¼ teaspoon ground pepper

*1 oz (30 g) chopped fresh
basil, oregano, or parsley*

❖ Peel, seed, and finely chop the fresh tomatoes (if using). In a large saucepan, heat the oil over medium heat. Add the fresh or undrained canned tomatoes, garlic, salt, sugar, and pepper. Bring to a boil. Reduce the heat and simmer, uncovered, for about 20 minutes, or until thickened to the desired consistency.

❖ Place half the sauce in a food processor or blender and process until smooth. Transfer to a bowl and repeat with the remaining sauce. Return all of the sauce to the pan and stir in the basil, oregano, or parsley. Cook for 5 minutes more.

❖ This sauce keeps well, covered, in the refrigerator for up to 1 week.

spinach gnocchi
with gorgonzola

**serves 6 as an appetizer,
or 4 as a main course**

*1¼ lb (625 g) fresh spinach, stems
removed, or 1 package (10 oz/315 g)
frozen leaf spinach, thawed*

*1 lb 10 oz (800 g) potatoes, unpeeled,
cut into large pieces*

*2½ cups (12½ oz/390 g) all-purpose
(plain) flour, plus ½ cup (2½ oz/75 g) extra,
for dusting*

1 extra-large (70–75 g) egg

GORGONZOLA SAUCE

*2 cups (16 fl oz/500 ml) heavy
(double) cream*

*2 oz (60 g) sweet Gorgonzola
cheese, crumbled*

3 tablespoons fruity Italian white wine

*1 teaspoon Cognac or other
brandy (optional)*

salt and ground white pepper

pinch of grated nutmeg

❖ If using fresh spinach for the gnocchi, place it on a steamer rack over boiling water. Cover and steam until the spinach is wilted and tender, 3–4 minutes. Drain and allow to cool.

❖ Use your hands to squeeze the cooled or thawed, frozen spinach to remove the excess liquid. Place the spinach in a food processor and process until smooth. Transfer to paper towels, squeeze to remove any remaining liquid, and set aside.

❖ Place the potatoes on a steamer rack over boiling water, cover, and steam until tender, 8–10 minutes. While they are still hot, peel the potatoes and then put them through a ricer onto a clean work surface to form a wide, low mound. Sprinkle with the 2½ cups (12½ oz/390 g) flour and then quickly and gently "fluff" the potato and flour together using your fingertips.

❖ Place the spinach on top and, using a fork or your fingertips, begin to work it into the potato mixture to form a dough. Crack the egg on top and lightly mix it in. Press the mixture together, then knead just until a dough forms.

❖ Clean the work surface and sprinkle with a little more flour. Divide the dough into 6 equal portions; cover 5 of the portions with a kitchen towel to prevent them drying out. Form the remaining portion into a log, ¾ inch (2 cm) in diameter. Cut the log crosswise into pieces ¾ inch (2 cm) wide. If the pieces are sticky, lightly coat them with some of the remaining flour. Repeat with the remaining portions of dough.

spinach gnocchi

❖ In a large saucepan of boiling salted water cook the gnocchi, stirring occasionally, until they are just cooked through, 12–15 minutes.

❖ Meanwhile, for the Gorgonzola sauce, bring the cream to a boil in a frying pan over high heat. Boil until slightly thickened, about 4 minutes. Stir in the cheese and reduce the heat to medium. Stir in the wine and simmer for 1 minute more. Stir in the brandy (if using). Season to taste with salt and pepper, and add the nutmeg. Stir gently to combine.

❖ Drain the gnocchi and add to the sauce. Toss well to coat and serve immediately.

food fact

Gorgonzola is a blue-vein, cow's milk cheese with a soft, creamy-white interior that is streaked with blue-green veins. It is matured in caves in northern Italy, where it has been made since at least the ninth century. There are two types: *Gorgonzola naturale* has a strong, rich, tangy flavor, while *gorgonzola dolcelatte* is slightly sweeter.

tomato-vegetable sauce

makes about 4 cups (32 fl oz/1 liter)

1 tablespoon olive oil

8 oz (250 g) fresh mushrooms, thinly sliced

1/2 cup (2 1/2 oz/75 g) chopped onion

2 cloves garlic, finely chopped

10 oz (315 g) shredded zucchini (courgettes)

15 oz (470 g) canned Italian-style chunky tomato sauce

1/2 cup (4 fl oz/125 ml) dry red wine

1 tablespoon chopped fresh sage

1/4 teaspoon salt

1/4 teaspoon pepper

❖ In a large frying pan heat the olive oil and cook the mushrooms, onion, and garlic, stirring constantly, for 5 minutes. Add the zucchini and cook for 5 minutes, or until the vegetables are tender.

❖ Add the tomato sauce, wine, sage, salt, and pepper. Bring to a boil, then reduce the heat and simmer, uncovered, stirring often, for 10–15 minutes, or until thickened to the desired consistency.

sun-dried tomatoes

30 ripe plum (Roma)
tomatoes, halved
lengthways

MARINADE (OPTIONAL)

equal parts water and
white wine vinegar,
to cover

1 clove garlic,
finely chopped

2 bay leaves

6 black peppercorns

1 tablespoon pine nuts

1 small dried red
chile, crumbled

½ cup (4 fl oz/125 ml)
virgin olive oil

❖ Place the tomatoes, cut-side up, on window screens covered with cheesecloth in a sunny location. Bring the screens inside at night. After about 4 days the tomatoes will be leathery and pliable. Place the tomatoes on a baking sheet and heat in an oven preheated to 160°F (70°C/Gas Mark ½) for 10–15 minutes to kill any insects.

❖ Place the dried tomatoes in airtight glass jars. If not adding the marinade, store in a cool, dark place (the refrigerator is ideal) for up to 6 months.

❖ For the marinade, soak the dried tomatoes in a mixing bowl in equal parts of water and vinegar for about 15 minutes, or until they are soft and chewy.

❖ Drain the tomatoes on paper towels and pat dry. Use tongs to transfer to airtight glass jars.

❖ Combine the remaining marinade ingredients and pour over the tomatoes. Clean the rims of the jars, seal tightly, and label. Set aside for about 1 week before using to develop the flavors. Store in the refrigerator for up to 1 month after opening.

fettuccine with creamy
parmesan
sauce

serves 2

⅓ cup (2½ fl oz/80 ml) light
(single) or heavy (double) cream

2 tablespoons margarine
or butter

4 oz (125 g) dried or 8 oz
(250 g) fresh tomato, herb,
or plain fettuccine

1½ oz (45 g) grated
Parmesan cheese

¼ teaspoon salt

1 small clove garlic,
finely chopped

1 tablespoon chopped fresh
basil or parsley (optional)

ground black pepper (optional)

❖ Bring the cream and margarine or butter to room temperature (this will take about 40 minutes).

❖ In a large saucepan of boiling salted water cook the pasta until al dente; drain.

❖ Return the pasta to the pan and add the cream, margarine or butter, cheese, salt, and garlic. Toss gently until the pasta is well coated. Sprinkle with basil or parsley and pepper, if desired. Serve immediately.

springtime carbonara

serves 4 as an appetizer

We call this "springtime" because vegetables replace the bacon used in traditional carbonara. However, with so many fresh vegetables now available all year round, you can enjoy this delicious carbonara in winter, too.

4 oz (125 g) baby carrots

5 oz (155 g) frozen peas or shelled fresh peas

4 oz (125 g) asparagus, trimmed, cut into 2-inch (5-cm) pieces

6 oz (185 g) dried or 12 oz (375 g) fresh spaghetti, fettuccine, or other ribbon pasta

1 egg, beaten lightly

1 cup (8 fl oz/250 ml) light (single) cream

2 tablespoons margarine or butter

1/2 cup (2 oz/60 g) grated Parmesan cheese

2 tablespoons chopped fresh chives or green (spring) onions

pepper

✥ In a medium saucepan cook the carrots in a small amount of boiling water for 10 minutes. Add the peas and asparagus. Cook for 5 minutes more, or until the vegetables are just tender. Drain.

✥ Meanwhile, in a large saucepan of boiling salted water cook the pasta until al dente.

✥ In a medium saucepan combine the egg, cream, and margarine or butter. Cook, stirring, over medium heat until the mixture just coats the back of a metal spoon, 3–4 minutes. Remove from the heat and stir in the cheese and chives or green onions.

✥ Drain the pasta and return to the saucepan. Add the cooked vegetables, then pour the egg mixture over the top and toss to combine. Sprinkle with pepper and serve immediately.

recipe variations

There are many different combinations of vegetables that would work well in this dish. Try using broccoli, zucchini (courgettes), squash, green beans, fava (broad) beans, cauliflower, wild mushrooms, and/or bell peppers (capsicums).

fettuccine
with gorgonzola and tarragon

serves 4 as an appetizer, or 2 as a main course

*4 oz (125 g) dried or 8 oz
(250 g) fresh spinach fettuccine*

1 tablespoon butter

*2 oz (60 g) crumbled
Gorgonzola cheese*

*¼ cup (2 fl oz/60 ml) light
(single) cream*

*2 tablespoons chopped fresh
tarragon or 1½ teaspoons
dried tarragon, crushed*

pinch of ground white pepper

*¼ cup (1 oz/30 g) grated
Parmesan cheese, plus extra
to serve (optional)*

*2 tablespoons chopped toasted
pecans or walnuts*

❖ In a large saucepan of boiling salted water cook the pasta until al dente; drain and return to the saucepan.

❖ Meanwhile, in a small saucepan melt the butter. Add the Gorgonzola, cream, tarragon, and pepper. Cook over medium heat, stirring, until the cheese melts and the mixture is smooth and heated through. Stir in the Parmesan.

❖ Pour the sauce over the pasta and gently toss until the pasta is coated. Sprinkle with the nuts and serve immediately, with extra Parmesan cheese, if desired.

aglio e olio
with fresh sage

serves 4 as an appetizer, or 2 as a main course

4 oz (125 g) dried mafalde, spaghetti, or other ribbon pasta or 8 oz (250 g) fresh fettuccine

2 tablespoons olive oil

2 cloves garlic, finely chopped

1 tablespoon chopped fresh sage or ½ teaspoon dried sage, crushed

salt and pepper

grated Parmesan cheese (optional)

❖ In a large saucepan of boiling salted water cook the pasta until al dente; drain and return to the pan.

❖ Meanwhile, heat the oil in a small saucepan over medium heat. Add the garlic and sage and cook, stirring, for 1 minute.

❖ Add the sage mixture to the hot pasta and toss to combine. Season to taste with salt and pepper. Serve immediately, sprinkled with Parmesan cheese, if desired.

straw and hay
with mushrooms

serves 4

4 oz (125 g) dried plain
fettuccine

4 oz (125 g) dried spinach
fettuccine

3 tablespoons margarine
or butter

1 oz (30 g) sliced green
(spring) onions

4 oz (125 g) finely chopped red
or green bell pepper (capsicum)

6 oz (185 g) fresh shiitake
mushrooms, sliced

1 cup (8 oz/250 ml) light
(single) or heavy (double) cream

¼ cup (1 oz/30 g) grated
Parmesan cheese

pepper

❖ In a large saucepan of boiling salted water cook the
pasta until al dente; drain and return to the saucepan.

❖ Meanwhile, in a large frying pan melt the margarine
or butter over medium-high heat. Cook the green
onions and bell pepper, stirring often, for 2 minutes.
Add the mushrooms and cook, stirring often, for a
further 2 minutes, or until the vegetables are tender.
Stir in the cream and heat through, but do not boil.

❖ Pour the mushroom mixture over the hot pasta and
toss to coat. Add the cheese and toss to combine.
Sprinkle with pepper and serve immediately.

toasted vermicelli
with fresh salsa

serves 2

2 tablespoons olive oil

5 oz (155 g) vermicelli or capellini,
broken into ½-inch (13-mm) pieces

2 oz (60 g) chopped onion

1 clove garlic, thinly sliced

2 tomatoes, peeled, seeded, and chopped

2 cups (16 fl oz/500 ml) chicken stock

3 small fresh chiles, seeded
and thinly sliced

½ teaspoon dried oregano, crushed

¼ teaspoon ground cumin

¼ teaspoon salt

2 tablespoons chopped
cilantro (fresh coriander)

chopped tomatoes (optional), for garnish

❖ In a large frying pan heat the olive oil.
Cook the pasta, onion, and garlic, stirring,
for 5 minutes, or until the pasta is golden
and onion is tender.

❖ Gently stir in the tomatoes, stock, chiles,
oregano, cumin, and salt. Bring to a boil,
then reduce heat and simmer, uncovered,
for 8 minutes, or until the pasta is al dente.
Stir in the cilantro. Serve garnished with
chopped tomatoes, if desired.

pesto pasta
with vegetables

serves 2

¼ cup (2 fl oz/60 ml) Pesto
(page 65)

8 oz (250 g) tiny new potatoes

6 oz (185 g) green beans

4 oz (125 g) radiatori, fusilli,
or other shaped pasta

1–2 tablespoons water

2 tablespoons grated
Parmesan cheese

❖ Prepare the pesto as directed. Set aside.

❖ Cut the smallest potatoes in half and the rest into bite-sized pieces. Cut the beans into 2-inch (5-cm) pieces. In a medium saucepan cook the potatoes and beans in a small amount of boiling salted water for about 10 minutes, or until tender. Drain well.

❖ Meanwhile, in a large saucepan of boiling salted water cook the pasta until al dente. Drain and return the pasta to the pan. Add the potatoes and beans.

❖ In a small mixing bowl combine the pesto and enough of the water to make a sauce consistency. Add the pesto mixture and Parmesan to the pasta and vegetables and toss to coat. Serve immediately.

three-cheese linguine with black olives

serves 4

8 oz (250 g) dried or 1 lb (500 g) fresh linguine

2 tablespoons olive oil

2 tablespoons butter

2 tablespoons finely grated pecorino romano or Parmesan cheese

½ cup (2 oz/60 g) grated Cheddar cheese

½ cup (2 oz/60 g) grated mozzarella cheese

¾ cup (3 oz/90 g) pitted, small, whole black olives

finely chopped fresh parsley, for garnish

❖ In a large saucepan of boiling salted water cook the pasta until al dente. Drain well and transfer to a mixing bowl. Add the olive oil, butter, cheeses, and olives. Toss to combine. Serve immediately, garnished with the chopped fresh parsley.

penne with neapolitan sauce

serves 2–3

A tiny dash of anchovy paste helps give the sauce for this pasta dish the inimitable flavor of southern Italian cooking.

1 tablespoon olive oil

1½ oz (45 g) finely chopped onion

2 cloves garlic, finely chopped

1¾ lb (875 g) canned peeled tomatoes, chopped

2 tablespoons chopped fresh oregano or 2 teaspoons dried oregano, crushed

2 tablespoons tomato paste

1 tablespoon capers, drained and rinsed

1 teaspoon sugar

1 teaspoon anchovy paste

⅛–¼ teaspoon cayenne pepper

6 oz (185 g) penne, rigatoni, or other dried shaped pasta

1½ oz (45 g) kalamata olives, pitted and chopped

3 tablespoons chopped fresh parsley

⬖ In a large saucepan heat the olive oil. Cook the onion and garlic, stirring often, until the onion is tender. Stir in the undrained tomatoes, oregano, tomato paste, capers, sugar, anchovy paste, and cayenne pepper. Bring to a boil, then reduce the heat and simmer, uncovered, for about 20 minutes, or until thickened to the desired consistency.

⬖ Meanwhile, in a large saucepan of boiling salted water cook the pasta until al dente; drain and return the pasta to the saucepan.

⬖ Add the tomato mixture and olives to the pasta and toss to coat. Serve sprinkled with parsley.

food fact

Kalamata olives are Greek in origin. The black, oval-shaped olives are treated with brine and are then cured in a mixture of oil and red wine vinegar. Anchovy paste is a commercially prepared mixture of anchovies, vinegar, spices, and water.

broccoli and pasta in
garlic butter

serves 2

4 oz (125 g) ruote, conchiglie,
or other dried shaped pasta

4 oz (125 g) broccoli or
cauliflower florets

1 tablespoon chopped fresh
basil or ½ teaspoon dried
basil, crushed

2 tablespoons butter

2 tablespoons olive oil

2 cloves garlic,
halved lengthways

1 oz (30 g) grated pecorino
romano or Parmesan cheese

ground pepper (optional)

❖ In a large saucepan of boiling salted water cook the pasta until al dente; drain well.

❖ Meanwhile, in a medium saucepan cook the broccoli or cauliflower florets and basil in a small amount of boiling salted water, covered, for 6–8 minutes or until tender crisp. Drain well.

❖ In a large frying pan heat the butter and oil. Add the garlic and cook, stirring occasionally, for 5 minutes, or until golden. Remove the garlic and discard.

❖ Add the broccoli or cauliflower florets to the butter mixture and toss to coat; heat through. Add the hot cooked pasta and cheese and toss to combine. If desired, season with pepper. Serve immediately.

white cheese
macaroni

serves 2

4 oz (125 g) elbow macaroni

1 large clove garlic, cut
lengthwise into slivers

1/3 cup (2½ fl oz/80 ml) milk

1 tablespoon margarine
or butter

1 cup (4 oz/125 g) shredded
sharp white Cheddar cheese

¼ teaspoon ground white
or black pepper

1 tablespoon chopped fresh
parsley, for garnish

❖ Bring a large saucepan of salted water to the boil.
Add the pasta and garlic slivers. Boil, uncovered,
stirring occasionally, until the pasta is al dente. Drain
and return the pasta and garlic to the saucepan.

❖ Add the milk to the saucepan and cook over low
heat for 2–3 minutes, or until all the milk is absorbed.
Add the margarine or butter, cheese, and pepper. Stir
gently until the cheese melts. Serve immediately,
garnished with chopped parsley.

vegetable lasagna

serves 6

If you would like to use fresh artichokes in this recipe, first trim the stems, then break off the tough outer leaves until only soft ones with a hint of yellow remain. Trim the leaves to 1 inch (2.5 cm). Cut the artichokes in half, then use a teaspoon to scoop out and discard the hairy chokes. Place in a bowl filled with water and the juice of 1 lemon until ready to use. To cook, place in simmering water for 10 minutes, or until tender.

6 lasagna noodles

VEGETABLES

9 oz (280 g) package frozen artichoke hearts

1 tablespoon margarine or butter

8 oz (250 g) sliced fresh mushrooms

5 oz (155 g) shredded carrot

SAUCE

1 tablespoon margarine or butter

1½ oz (45 g) sliced green (spring) onion

2 cloves garlic, finely chopped

¼ cup (1 oz/30 g) all-purpose (plain) flour

¼ teaspoon ground pepper

1 cup (8 fl oz/250 ml) light (single)
cream or milk

3/4 cup (6 fl oz/185 ml) chicken stock

FILLING

10 oz (315 g) frozen chopped spinach,
thawed and drained

8 oz (250 g) cream-style cottage
cheese, drained

1/4 cup (1 oz/30 g) grated Parmesan cheese

TOPPING

1/4 cup (1 oz/30 g) grated Parmesan cheese

❖ In a large saucepan of boiling salted
water cook the pasta until al dente. Drain,
rinse with cold water, and drain again.

❖ For the vegetables, cook the artichoke
hearts according to package directions.
Drain and chop. In a large frying pan
melt the margarine or butter. Cook the
mushrooms and carrot, stirring often, for
3 minutes, or until tender. Stir in the
chopped artichoke hearts and set aside.

❖ For the sauce, in a medium saucepan
melt the margarine or butter. Cook the
green onion and garlic, stirring often, until
tender. Stir in the flour and pepper. Add the
cream or milk, and stock. Cook, stirring,
until the mixture boils and thickens. Remove
from the heat and set aside.

❖ For the filling, in a bowl combine the
spinach, cottage cheese, and Parmesan.

vegetable lasagna

❖ Preheat an oven to 350°F (180°C/Gas Mark 4). To assemble the lasagna, grease an 8-cup (2-qt/2-l) rectangular baking dish. Arrange 3 of the noodles in the base of the dish and spread with half of the filling. Top with half of the vegetables, then half of the sauce. Repeat to make another layer of each.

❖ Bake the lasagna, covered, for 35 minutes. Uncover and sprinkle with the topping. Bake for a further 5–10 minutes, or until the mixture is heated through. Set aside for 10 minutes before serving.

recipe variations

For the topping, you can use grated Cheddar, mozzarella, or fontina cheese, if desired. For a crunchy topping, combine the cheese with fine dried bread crumbs.

potato
gnocchi
with parmesan

serves 4

1½ lb (750 g) all-purpose potatoes, peeled and quartered

1 egg, lightly beaten

1½ cups (6 oz/185 g) all-purpose (plain) flour, or as needed, plus extra for kneading

SAUCE

½ cup (4 oz/125 g) butter

1 clove garlic, crushed

1 cup (8 fl oz/250 ml) light (single) cream

½ cup (2 oz/60 g) grated Parmesan cheese

2 tablespoons finely chopped fresh sage

fresh sage leaves, for garnish

❖ Cook the potatoes in boiling salted water until tender; drain. Push the potatoes through a fine-mesh sieve into a large bowl. Stir in the egg and enough flour to form a soft dough. Turn onto a floured surface and knead until smooth. Shape teaspoonfuls of dough into balls and roll each down the tines of a floured fork. In a large saucepan of boiling salted water cook the gnocchi, in batches, until they rise to the surface.

❖ For the sauce, melt the butter in a saucepan. Add the garlic and cook, stirring, for 1 minute. Stir in the cream. Bring to a boil, then reduce heat and simmer for 2 minutes. Add the cheese and stir until it melts and the sauce thickens. Stir in the chopped sage. Spoon over the gnocchi and serve garnished with sage leaves.

mushroom-filled **ravioli**

serves 6 as an appetizer

A mixture of several types
of mushrooms will add
a deep, woody flavor to
the ravioli filling. This dish
makes a beautiful first
course or light supper. For
an hors d'oeuvre, serve the
ravioli in a shallow dish
with toothpicks.

2 portions (each 8 oz/250 g) Spinach Pasta (page 305)

FILLING

1 tablespoon margarine or butter

4 oz (125 g) finely chopped fresh mushrooms

1½ oz (45 g) finely chopped onion

1 clove garlic, finely chopped

1 egg, beaten

¼ cup (1 oz/30 g) seasoned fine dried bread crumbs

¼ cup (1 oz/30 g) grated Parmesan cheese

¼ teaspoon dried thyme, crushed

SAUCE

1 cup (8 fl oz/250 ml) heavy (double) cream

fresh thyme leaves (optional), for garnish

✤ Preheat an oven to 300°F (150°C/Gas Mark 2).

✤ Prepare the spinach pasta as directed, except roll each portion of dough into an 8- x 12-inch (20- x 30-cm) rectangle. Cover and set aside.

✤ For the filling, melt the margarine or butter in a large frying pan. Cook the mushrooms, onion, and garlic for 5 minutes, or until tender. In a medium mixing bowl combine the egg, bread crumbs, cheese, and thyme. Stir in the mushroom mixture and set aside.

✤ Cut each pasta sheet into 4 strips, each 2 x 12 inches (5 x 30 cm) and brush with water. Place the filling on 1 pasta strip in 2-teaspoon amounts, each 2 inches (5 cm) apart, beginning 1 inch (2.5 cm) from the end of the strip. Top with a second pasta strip and press down gently around each mound of filling. Use a 2-inch (5-cm) ravioli wheel, square cookie cutter, or sharp knife to cut out the ravioli. Press the edges firmly to seal. Repeat with the remaining pasta strips and filling.

✤ For the sauce, heat the cream in a small saucepan over medium heat, stirring often, until it is boiling. Boil gently for 3–4 minutes.

✤ Meanwhile, bring a large saucepan of salted water to the boil. Add half of the ravioli and cook, stirring occasionally, until al dente. Use a slotted spoon to transfer to a greased casserole. Cover and keep warm in the oven while cooking the remaining ravioli. Pour the thickened cream over the ravioli, sprinkle with the thyme leaves, if desired, and serve immediately.

manicotti
with
roasted vegetables

serves 4–6

½ medium green bell pepper (capsicum)

½ medium red or orange
bell pepper (capsicum)

½ medium yellow bell pepper (capsicum)

½ medium onion

1 medium yellow squash

1 medium zucchini (courgette)

2 cloves garlic, peeled

1 tablespoon olive oil

1 quantity Herb and Tomato Sauce
(page 101) or 32 fl oz (1 liter)
purchased Italian-style tomato sauce

8–12 manicotti, or 16–24 other extra-large
pasta shells

2 eggs, lightly beaten

2 cups (8 oz/250 g) shredded
mozzarella cheese

1½ cups (12 oz/375 g) ricotta cheese

1½ oz (45 g) grated Parmesan cheese

2 tablespoons chopped fresh chives

¼ teaspoon ground white or black pepper

❖ Preheat an oven to 425°F (210°C/Gas Mark 5). Cut the bell peppers into bite-sized strips and cut the onion into small wedges. Cut the squash and zucchini into ¼-inch (6-mm) thick slices. In a 13- x 9- x 2-in (33- x 23- x 5-cm) baking dish combine the bell peppers, onion, squash, zucchini, and garlic. Drizzle with olive oil and bake, stirring once or twice, for 30 minutes, or until tender. Remove the garlic cloves. Reduce oven temperature to 350°F (180°C/Gas Mark 4).

❖ Meanwhile, if using the herb and tomato sauce, prepare as directed. Set aside. In a large saucepan of boiling salted water cook the pasta, stirring occasionally, until al dente. Drain, rinse under cold running water, and drain again.

❖ In a medium mixing bowl combine the eggs, mozzarella, ricotta, Parmesan, chives, and pepper. Divide the cheese mixture among the pasta shells and arrange them in a 12-cup (3-qt/3-1) rectangular baking dish. Pour the tomato sauce over the top. Arrange the roasted vegetables on top of the sauce. Bake, covered, for 35–40 minutes, or until heated through.

spinach cannelloni

serves 4

CANNELLONI

1 portion (4 oz/125 g) Homemade Pasta (page 305) or 6 purchased lasagna noodles

5 oz (155 g) fresh spinach or frozen chopped spinach, thawed

2 tablespoons olive oil

3–4 cloves garlic, peeled and quartered

1/4 cup (1 oz/30 g) grated Parmesan cheese

2 tablespoons fine dried bread crumbs

1/8 teaspoon cayenne pepper

2 teaspoons olive oil, extra

1 tablespoon grated Parmesan cheese, extra

SAUCE

1/2 cup (4 fl oz/125 ml) chicken stock

1 1/2 teaspoons cornstarch (cornflour)

1 teaspoon butter

1 tablespoon fresh lemon juice

1 tablespoon heavy (double) cream

1 1/2 oz (45 g) toasted pine nuts

❖ If using homemade pasta, prepare as directed. Cut into sixteen 3-inch (7.5-cm) squares, cover, and set aside. If using lasagna noodles, cook according to package directions; drain. Cut each noodle into 3 even pieces, place on a damp kitchen towel, cover, and set aside.

❖ Trim and wash the fresh spinach (if using); finely chop. In a large frying pan heat the olive oil over medium-high heat. Cook the garlic, stirring, for 30 seconds. Add the chopped fresh or thawed frozen spinach. Cook, stirring, for 1–2 minutes, or until the spinach is heated through. Drain in a colander, squeezing out the excess liquid. In a medium mixing bowl combine the spinach, cheese, bread crumbs, and cayenne pepper.

❖ Meanwhile, if using homemade pasta, cook the pasta in a large saucepan of boiling salted water, stirring occasionally, until al dente. Use a slotted spoon to carefully transfer to a colander. Rinse with cold water; drain well. Carefully lay the pasta on a damp kitchen towel.

❖ To assemble, place 1 scant tablespoon of spinach mixture along 1 end of each piece of pasta. Roll the pasta tightly around the filling to enclose. Place all the pasta rolls on a greased baking sheet, drizzle with the extra olive oil, and sprinkle with the extra cheese. Place under a broiler (griller), 6 inches (15 cm) from the heat, for 5 minutes, or until golden brown.

❖ Meanwhile, for the sauce, combine the stock and cornstarch in a small saucepan. Add the butter. Cook, stirring, until the mixture boils and thickens. Stir in the lemon juice and cream and heat through. Spoon over the cannelloni, sprinkle with the pine nuts, and serve.

potato and herb
dumplings
in tomato sauce

serves 4

1 1/2 lb (750 g) potatoes, peeled and cut into small pieces

1 egg

3 tablespoons all-purpose (plain) flour

2 tablespoons cornstarch (cornflour)

salt

2 teaspoons finely chopped fresh rosemary

2 tablespoons finely shredded fresh basil

2 tablespoons finely snipped fresh chives

SAUCE

1 tablespoon olive oil

1 large onion, chopped

1 clove garlic, crushed

2 x 13 1/2 oz (425 g) cans plum (Roma) tomatoes, mashed

1 tablespoon tomato paste

1 bay leaf

salt and ground pepper

1/3 cup (1 1/2 oz/45 g) grated Parmesan cheese

1/2 cup (1 oz/30 g) finely chopped fresh parsley

❖ Cook the potatoes in boiling salted water until tender. Drain, cool, and push them through a fine-mesh sieve or a ricer into a bowl. Add the egg, flour, cornstarch, and salt and mix until thoroughly combined. Combine the rosemary, basil, and chives in a small bowl. Roll the potato mixture into balls, using about 1½ teaspoons per ball. Press about 1 teaspoon of herbs into the center of each ball. Reshape each ball so that the potato mixture encloses the herbs. Refrigerate until ready to cook.

❖ For the sauce, heat the oil in a saucepan and cook the onion and garlic until the onion is soft. Stir in the undrained tomatoes, tomato paste, and bay leaf. Bring the mixture to a boil, then reduce the heat and simmer for 30 minutes or until the sauce thickens. Remove the bay leaf and season to taste with salt and pepper.

❖ Meanwhile, preheat an oven to 250°F (120°C/Gas Mark 1). Combine the cheese and parsley on a plate. In a large saucepan of boiling salted water cook the potato dumplings, a few at a time, for about 8 minutes, or until cooked through. Use a slotted spoon to remove; drain and then roll in the cheese mixture. Place on a baking sheet in preheated oven to keep warm while cooking the remaining dumplings. Spoon the sauce onto serving dishes and arrange the dumplings on top.

pasta
with
poultry

fettuccine
with chicken,
tomatoes, and arugula

serves 4

12 oz (375 g) cooked chicken meat, cut into bite-sized pieces

2 oz (60 g) drained, oil-packed sun-dried tomatoes

12–16 cherry tomatoes, halved

½ small red (Spanish) onion, thinly sliced into rings

1 cup (8 fl oz/250 ml) thick (double) cream

salt and ground pepper

8 oz (250 g) dried or 1 lb (500 g) fresh fettuccine

4 tablespoons pesto, home-made (page 65) or purchased

1 bunch arugula (rocket), washed, picked over, and dried

Parmesan shavings, to serve

❖ In a frying pan, combine the chicken, sun-dried and cherry tomatoes, the onion, cream, and salt and pepper to taste. Bring to a simmer, then reduce the heat to low and cook, stirring occasionally, until the chicken is heated through and the sauce is bubbling and slightly thickened, about 5 minutes.

❖ Meanwhile, cook the pasta in plenty of boiling salted water until al dente. Drain, return to the pot, add the sauce and pesto, and toss to combine.

❖ Arrange the arugula around the edges of 4 serving plates. Pile the pasta mixture into the center of each plate and serve immediately, spinkled with Parmesan.

fettuccine
with chicken, avocado, and rosemary

serves 6

3 tablespoons butter

2 large onions, finely diced

¼ cup (2 fl oz/60 ml) brandy

¼ cup (1 oz/30 g) all-purpose (plain) flour

1 teaspoon salt

1 teaspoon paprika

1 tablespoon fresh rosemary or
1½ teaspoons dried rosemary

ground black pepper

2 cups (16 fl oz/500 ml) chicken stock

1¼ cups (10 fl oz/310 ml) sour cream

½ cup (4 fl oz/125 ml) milk

1½ lb (750 g) cooked chicken meat,
cut into bite-sized pieces

1 lb (500 g) fettuccine

1 large avocado, peeled,
stone removed, flesh diced

In a large saucepan melt the butter. Add the onions and cook gently until they are soft and begin to brown. Add the brandy and simmer until it is almost absorbed. Gradually add the flour, stirring constantly, until the mixture thickens. Stir in the salt, paprika, rosemary, and pepper. Cook gently for about 2 minutes. Gradually stir in the chicken stock and bring the mixture to a boil. Boil gently for 3 minutes.

Remove the pan from the heat and gradually beat in the sour cream and then the milk. Stir in the chicken. Simmer gently over low heat for 15 minutes.

Meanwhile, in a large saucepan of boiling salted water cook the pasta until al dente; drain.

Add the avocado to the sauce and fold through.

Divide the pasta among serving dishes, top with the sauce and serve immediately.

recipe hint

The color of an avocado's skin differs from one variety to the next, so is not a good indicator of ripeness. Rather, gently feel the avocado. If it yields slightly to the touch, it is ripe. If it is very soft, it may be over-ripe.

turkey tetrazzini

serves 4

According to culinary
folklore, the opera singer
Luisa Tetrazzini inspired the
original version of this dish
almost a century ago.

8 (1 oz/30 g) sun-dried tomatoes (not oil-packed)

6 oz (185 g) dried spaghetti, vermicelli, or capellini,
or 12 oz (375 g) fresh linguine or other ribbon pasta

3 tablespoons margarine or butter

5 oz (155 g) stemmed and sliced fresh shiitake
mushrooms or white mushrooms

1/4 cup (1 oz/30 g) all-purpose (plain) flour

pinch of ground nutmeg

1 1/2 cups (12 fl oz/375 ml) light (single) cream or milk

1 cup (8 fl oz/250 ml) chicken stock

15 oz (470 g) chopped cooked turkey or chicken meat

2 tablespoons dry sherry

1/4 cup (1 oz/30 g) grated Parmesan cheese

1 oz (30 g) sliced (flaked) almonds

❖ Place the sun-dried tomatoes in a small bowl. Add enough hot water to cover and set aside for 10–15 minutes, or until softened. Drain and pat dry. Chop the tomatoes and set aside.

❖ Preheat an oven to 350°F (180°C/Gas Mark 4). In a large saucepan of boiling salted water cook the pasta until al dente (10–12 minutes for spaghetti, 5–7 minutes for vermicelli or capellini, or 1–2 minutes for fresh pasta). Drain.

❖ Meanwhile, in a large saucepan melt the margarine or butter. Add the mushrooms and cook, stirring often, until tender. Stir in the flour and nutmeg. Add the cream or milk, and stock. Cook, stirring, until the mixture boils and thickens. Stir in the turkey or chicken, sherry, and chopped tomatoes. Add the cooked pasta and toss to coat.

❖ Transfer the mixture to an 8-cup (2-qt/2-l) rectangular baking dish. Sprinkle with the cheese and almonds. Bake for 20 minutes, or until heated through. Serve immediately.

pasta with chicken livers

serves 4

Italian cooks, particularly
Florentines, love chicken
livers. One of the many good
culinary uses to which they
are put is this rich and
hearty sauce for pasta. The
sauce is served with shaped
pasta so you can pick up
a delicious morsel of
liver with each bite.

8 oz (250 g) farfalle (bow-tie pasta)

2 tablespoons margarine or butter

12 oz (375 g) chicken livers, cut in halves

1 oz (30 g) sliced green (spring) onion

1½ oz (45 g) chopped green bell pepper (capsicum)

1½ oz (45 g) chopped red bell pepper (capsicum)

½ cup (2 oz/60 g) all-purpose (plain) flour

salt and ground pepper

1¼ cups (10 fl oz/315 ml) chicken stock

⅔ cup (5 fl oz/160 ml) light (single) cream or milk

1 tablespoon chopped fresh sage

❖ In a large saucepan of boiling salted water cook the pasta until al dente. Drain and return to the saucepan.

❖ Meanwhile, in a large frying pan melt the margarine or butter over medium-high heat. Add the chicken livers and cook, turning as needed, for 4–5 minutes, or until the centers are just slightly pink. Use a slotted spoon to remove from the pan; cover to keep warm.

❖ Add the green onion and bell pepper to the frying pan and cook, stirring often, for 2–3 minutes, or until tender. Stir in the flour, salt, and pepper. Add the stock, cream or milk, and sage. Cook, stirring, until the mixture boils and thickens. Boil, stirring, for 1 minute. Add the sauce to the hot cooked pasta and toss to coat. Add the chicken livers and toss gently to combine. Serve immediately.

recipe hint

Other pasta shapes that could be used in this recipe include fusilli (pasta spirals), pasta shells, macaroni, or any other small, shaped, dried pasta to which the sauce can cling.

serves 4

½ cup (4 oz/125 ml) chicken stock

1 tablespoon Worcestershire sauce

*1 tablespoon chopped fresh oregano
or 1 teaspoon dried oregano, crushed*

*2 teaspoons chopped fresh thyme
or ½ teaspoon dried thyme, crushed*

2 teaspoons cornstarch (cornflour)

⅛ teaspoon crushed chile flakes

*12 oz (375 g) skinless, boneless
chicken breast halves or thighs,
cut into bite-sized pieces*

*3 slices bacon, cut into
½-inch (12-mm) pieces*

1 tablespoon olive oil

*1 red bell pepper (capsicum), cut into
¾-inch (2-cm) pieces*

*1 medium onion, thinly sliced and
separated into rings*

2 cloves garlic, finely chopped

*9 oz (280 g) canned or thawed
frozen artichoke hearts, quartered*

hot cooked penne pasta

❖ In a small bowl, combine the stock, Worcestershire sauce, oregano, thyme, cornstarch, and chile flakes. Add chicken, toss to coat, and set aside to marinate.

❖ In a wok or large frying pan cook the bacon until crisp; drain on paper towels. Drain fat from pan and wipe clean with paper towels. Add the oil and warm it over medium-high heat. Add the bell pepper and onion and stir-fry for 2 minutes, or until tender crisp. Add the garlic and stir-fry for 15 seconds. Remove vegetables from the wok.

❖ Drain the chicken, reserving the marinade. Add chicken to the wok and stir-fry for 2–3 minutes, or until just cooked through. Push chicken to edges of wok. Stir marinade and pour into center of wok. Stir until mixture boils and thickens. Stir in the cooked vegetables and artichokes and cook until heated through.

❖ Spoon sauce over the pasta. Sprinkle with the bacon and serve immediately.

chicken
with artichokes

pasta
with turkey
and tomatoes

serves 4

2 tablespoons olive oil

2 lb (1 kg) plum (Roma) tomatoes, peeled and chopped,
or 30 oz (940 g) canned plum (Roma) tomatoes,
chopped, with juice

2 cloves garlic, finely chopped

½ teaspoon sugar

salt and pepper

½ cup (4 fl oz/125 ml) heavy (double) cream

12 oz (375 g) fully cooked smoked turkey breast,
cut into 2- x ¼-inch (5-cm x 6-mm) strips

2 oz (60 g) drained oil-packed sun-dried tomatoes, chopped

2 tablespoons chopped fresh parsley

8 oz (250 g) dried linguine or fettuccine, or
1 lb (500 g) fresh linguine or fettuccine

¼ cup (1 oz/30 g) grated Parmesan cheese (optional)

❖ In a large frying pan heat the oil over medium heat. Add the tomatoes (and their juice, if using canned tomatoes), the garlic, sugar, and salt and pepper to taste. Bring to a boil. Reduce heat and boil gently, uncovered, stirring occasionally, for 15 minutes or until the mixture thickens. Gradually add the cream, stirring constantly. Stir in the turkey and sun-dried tomatoes; heat through. Remove from heat and stir in the parsley.

❖ Meanwhile, in a large saucepan of boiling salted water cook the pasta until al dente (8–10 minutes for dried pasta, 1–2 minutes for fresh pasta); drain.

❖ Spoon the sauce over the pasta. Serve immediately, topped with cheese, if desired.

chicken orecchiette

serves 4

2 tablespoons butter

4 skinless, boneless
chicken breast halves
(1 lb/500 g total)

salt and ground
black pepper

1½ oz (45 g) sliced
fresh mushrooms

1 oz (30 g) finely
chopped shallots

¼ cup (2 fl oz/60 ml) dry
white wine

1 cup (8 fl oz/250 ml) chicken stock

2 tablespoons all-purpose
(plain) flour

2 teaspoons chopped
fresh thyme or ½ teaspoon
dried thyme, crushed

1 bay leaf

3 tablespoons heavy (double) cream

8 oz (250 g) orecchiette or
other short pasta

❖ In a large frying pan melt the butter over medium heat. Add the chicken and cook, turning once, for 10–12 minutes total, or until just cooked through. Sprinkle with salt and pepper, transfer to a large plate, cover, and keep warm.

❖ In the same frying pan cook the mushrooms and shallots for 3 minutes, or until tender. Spoon over the chicken; keep warm. Add the white wine to the pan, stirring to dislodge the browned bits on the base of the pan.

❖ Stir together the stock, flour, thyme, and bay leaf. Add to the pan and stir just until the mixture boils and thickens. Boil for 2 minutes, then stir in the cream. Remove the bay leaf and season to taste with salt and pepper.

❖ Meanwhile, cook pasta in boiling salted water until al dente; drain. Divide pasta between 4 serving plates. Top with chicken, mushrooms and shallots, and sauce. Serve at once.

chili spaghetti
with beans

serves 4–6

8 oz (250 g) dried spaghetti
or linguine, or 1 lb (500 g)
fresh ribbon pasta

MEAT SAUCE

1 lb (500 g) lean ground
(minced) chicken, turkey,
or beef

½ cup (2 oz/60 g) chopped
yellow onion

1 clove garlic, finely chopped

1 lb (500 g) ripe plum (Roma)
tomatoes, peeled, seeded, and
chopped, or canned peeled
tomatoes, chopped

1 cup (8 oz/250 g) canned
or bottled Italian-style
tomato sauce

¼ cup (2 fl oz/60 ml)
chicken stock

1 tablespoon red wine vinegar

1 tablespoon chile powder

½ teaspoon ground allspice

¼ teaspoon ground cinnamon

¼ teaspoon salt

⅛ teaspoon cayenne pepper

TOPPINGS

1 lb (500 g) canned cannellini
beans, rinsed

1 oz (30 g) thinly sliced
green (spring) onions

½ cup (2 oz/60 g)
grated Cheddar cheese or
¼ cup (1 oz/30 g) grated
Parmesan cheese

❖ In a large, preferably nonstick, frying pan cook the ground meat, onion, and garlic for 5 minutes, or until the meat is browned and onion is tender. Drain off fat. Stir in the fresh or undrained canned tomatoes, tomato sauce, chicken stock, vinegar, chile powder, allspice, cinnamon, salt, and cayenne pepper. Bring to a boil, then reduce heat and simmer, uncovered, stirring occasionally, for 15–20 minutes, or until the sauce is reduced to the desired consistency.

❖ Meanwhile, in a large saucepan of boiling salted water cook the pasta until al dente (8–12 minutes for dried pasta, 1–2 minutes for fresh pasta). Drain.

❖ To serve, heat the cannellini beans in a small saucepan; drain. Top the hot cooked pasta with the meat sauce, beans, green onions, and cheese. Serve immediately.

147

chicken
cannelloni

serves 4

1 portion (4 oz/125 g) Homemade
Pasta (pages 304–305)

1½ cups (12 fl oz/375 ml) Herb and
Tomato Sauce (page 101), or purchased
Italian-style tomato sauce

PARMESAN SAUCE

¼ cup (2 oz/60 g) butter

¼ cup (1 oz/30 g) all-purpose
(plain) flour

¼ teaspoon salt

⅛ teaspoon ground white pepper

1½ cups (12 fl oz/375 ml) milk

1½ oz (45 g) grated Parmesan cheese

3 tablespoons sour cream

CHICKEN FILLING

1 tablespoon olive oil

8 oz (250 g) skinless, boneless chicken
breast halves, chopped

½ cup (2 oz/60 g) chopped onion

1 cup (1 oz/30 g) chopped fresh parsley

1 clove garlic, finely chopped

¼ teaspoon salt

⅛ teaspoon ground white pepper

2 oz (60 g) prosciutto or ham,
roughly chopped

1 tablespoon grated Parmesan cheese

chicken cannelloni

❖ Prepare the pasta as directed. Cut into sixteen 3-inch (7.5-cm) squares. Cover and set aside. Prepare the herb and tomato sauce as directed. Set aside.

❖ For the Parmesan sauce, in a small saucepan melt the butter. Stir in the flour, salt, and pepper. Add the milk and cook over medium heat, stirring, until the mixture boils and thickens. Stir in the cheese and sour cream. Set aside.

❖ For the chicken filling, in a large frying pan heat the oil. Add the chicken, onion, parsley, garlic, salt, and pepper. Cook for 5 minutes, or until the chicken is just cooked through and the onion is tender. Cool slightly. Place the chicken mixture and prosciutto or ham in a food processor or blender. Process or blend until finely chopped. Transfer to a medium bowl and stir in ¾ cup (6 fl oz/185 ml) of the Parmesan sauce.

❖ Preheat an oven to 350°F (180°C/Gas Mark 4). In a large saucepan of boiling salted water cook the pasta until al dente, about 3–4 minutes. Drain.

❖ Place a scant 2 tablespoons of chicken filling along one edge of each pasta square and roll the pasta tightly around the filling. Place in a greased 12-cup (3-qt/3-l) rectangular baking dish. Pour the remaining Parmesan sauce over half the pasta, and pour the herb and tomato sauce over the remaining pasta. Sprinkle with Parmesan cheese and bake for 30–35 minutes, or until heated through. Serve immediately.

spicy turkey pasta

serves 4–6

12 oz (375 g) ground (minced) turkey

½ cup (2 oz/60 g) chopped onion

1 clove garlic, finely chopped

13½ oz (425 g) tomato sauce

1 cup (8 fl oz/250 ml) water

2 tablespoons chopped cilantro
(fresh coriander) leaves

1 tablespoon tomato paste

½ teaspoon salt

½ teaspoon ground cumin

¼ teaspoon chile powder

¼ teaspoon ground coriander

⅛ teaspoon cayenne pepper

4 oz (125 g) elbow macaroni

8 oz (250 g) canned red
kidney beans, drained

1 cup (4 oz/125 g) shredded Provolone cheese

❖ In a large frying pan cook the turkey, onion, and garlic for 5 minutes, or until onion is soft. Drain off fat. Add tomato sauce, water, cilantro, tomato paste, salt, cumin, chile powder, ground coriander, and cayenne. Bring to a boil, then reduce heat, cover and simmer for 15 minutes.

❖ Preheat an oven to 350°F (180°C/ Gas Mark 4). Grease an 8-cup (2-qt/2-l) square baking dish. Layer half the uncooked macaroni, half the turkey mixture, half the beans, and half the cheese. Repeat layers.

❖ Cover and bake for 40 minutes. Uncover and bake for 5 minutes, or until pasta is tender.

chicken
with tomato–basil
spaghettini

serves 4

2 tablespoons olive oil

5 oz (155 g) prosciutto, sliced

4 skinless, boneless chicken breast halves, thickly sliced

1 tablespoon balsamic vinegar

TOMATO–BASIL SPAGHETTINI

1 lb (500 g) spaghettini

1 tablespoon extra virgin olive oil

2 cloves garlic, crushed

6 (about 3 lb/1.5 kg) large ripe tomatoes, peeled and finely chopped

⅓ cup (⅓ oz/10 g) chopped fresh basil

5 oz (155 g) bocconcini, cubed

½ cup (2 oz/60 g) grated Parmesan cheese

2 teaspoons sugar

¼ cup (1 oz/30 g) drained sun-dried tomatoes, sliced

salt and pepper

shredded Parmesan cheese, for garnish

shredded fresh basil, for garnish

✧ Heat the oil in a frying pan, add the prosciutto and cook until just crisp. Transfer to paper towels to drain. Reheat the pan and add the chicken. Cook, stirring, until the chicken is just tender. Add the vinegar and stir until chicken is well coated. Keep warm.

✧ For the tomato-basil spaghettini, cook the pasta in a large saucepan of boiling salted water until al dente. Drain and return to the saucepan.

✧ Meanwhile, heat the oil in a saucepan, add the garlic, tomatoes, and basil and simmer, uncovered, for about 10 minutes, or until mixture is pulpy. Stir in the cheeses, sugar, and sun-dried tomatoes. Season to taste with salt and pepper, and add to the spaghettini. Toss well.

✧ Serve the tomato-basil spaghettini with the chicken and prosciutto, sprinkled with shredded Parmesan and shredded basil.

recipe variations

The tomato–basil spaghettini can also be served on its own as a light meal, with crusty Italian bread, if desired.

The prosciutto can be replaced with bacon, if you prefer.

pasta *with* meat

spicy penne

serves 4

1 tablespoon bacon
drippings (lard)

1 onion, finely chopped

2 cloves garlic, finely chopped

3 oz (90 g) pancetta, diced

1¼ lb (625 g) ripe
tomatoes, puréed

salt

½ teaspoon chile powder

13 oz (410 g) penne

¾ cup (3 oz/90 g) grated
pecorino romano cheese

❖ Melt the bacon drippings in a large frying pan over medium heat. Add the onion and garlic and cook, stirring often, until soft, but not brown. Add the pancetta and cook, stirring often, for 2–3 minutes. Add the tomatoes, salt and chile powder. Stir for a few minutes over high heat, until the sauce is hot.

❖ In a large saucepan of boiling salted water cook the pasta until al dente; drain. Add to the sauce with half of the cheese and toss to combine. Serve accompanied by the remaining cheese.

orecchiette
with cauliflower sauce

serves 4

Orecchiette is a small, ear-shaped type of pasta that is perfect for holding a chunky sauce. If you don't have time to make your own, simply substitute purchased orecchiette or other shaped pasta.

2 cups (10 oz/315 g) fine-ground semolina (continental flour)

water, as needed

1 cauliflower, trimmed, cut into florets

1 cup (8 fl oz/250 ml) extra virgin olive oil

2 cloves garlic, peeled and bruised

1½ oz (45 g) pancetta, finely chopped

ground pepper

½ cup (1 oz/30 g) fresh bread crumbs, browned in oil

½ cup (2 oz/60 g) grated pecorino romano cheese

❖ Place the semolina in a mound on a work surface and make a well in the center. Gradually add enough water to knead to a smooth, thick dough. Cover with a damp kitchen towel and set aside for 30 minutes to rest.

❖ Divide the dough into 4 pieces and roll each into a log about 1 inch (2.5 cm) in diameter. Cut each log into slices less than ½ inch (1 cm) thick. Using the tip of a finger, gently press down on each slice with a forward motion to create the characteristic concave dumplings called orecchiette. Repeat with the remaining dough. Spread the orecchiette out on the work surface for 1 hour to dry before cooking.

❖ Cook the cauliflower in a large saucepan of boiling salted water for 10 minutes. Add the orecchiette and cook until they rise to the surface, a few minutes.

❖ Meanwhile, in a large frying pan, heat the olive oil and cook the garlic, stirring often, until golden. Discard the garlic. Add the pancetta and fry gently.

❖ Drain the orecchiette and cauliflower. Add to the frying pan and season with pepper, to taste. Add the bread crumbs and cheese. Toss to combine, and serve.

parma-style anolini

serves 6

Similar in shape to tortellini but completely different in substance, anolini are a source of gastronomic pride in Parma, Italy. This dish was originally reserved for special occasions when poor families budgeted to buy meat. The cooking juices from the meat are mixed with bread crumbs to make the stuffing, so that the meat can be served on its own as another course.

STOCK

½ capon or 1 chicken, about 3 lb (1.5 kg)

2 lb (1 kg) beef brisket

20 cups (5 qt/5 l) water

2 onions, each studded with 2 cloves

2 carrots

2 celery stalks

2 tablespoons salt

FILLING

2 cups (16 fl oz/500 ml) beef stock

1 tablespoon tomato purée

1 lb (500 g) beef round steak

2 oz (60 g) pancetta, cubed

3–4 cloves garlic, sliced

3 tablespoons butter

1/2 cup (4 fl oz/125 ml) olive oil

1 onion, finely chopped

salt and pepper

3 cups (24 fl oz/750 ml) dry red wine

1 celery stalk, sliced

1 carrot, sliced

3 cloves

6 tablespoons dried bread crumbs, toasted

1 1/2 cups (6 oz/185 g) grated
Parmesan cheese

pinch of ground nutmeg

2 eggs, beaten

PASTA

4 cups (1 lb/500 g) all-purpose (plain) flour

2 eggs plus 3 egg yolks, beaten together

1 tablespoon olive oil

pinch of salt

❖ For the stock, place the capon, beef, water, onions, carrots, celery, and salt in a large saucepan. Bring to a boil, then simmer, covered, for 2 hours. Remove the capon and beef; reserve. Strain the liquid and set aside. Discard the vegetables.

❖ For the filling, heat the beef stock and tomato purée in a saucepan; keep warm over low heat.

❖ Make small cuts in the beef steak and insert the pancetta cubes and sliced garlic. In a large saucepan heat the butter and olive oil. Add the onion and cook until softened. Add the beef steak, sprinkle with salt and pepper, and cook until browned on all sides. Add the wine, and enough beef-and-tomato stock mixture to cover the meat. Add celery, carrot, and cloves. Cover and cook over low heat for 3–4 hours, or until beef is cooked and juices have reduced.

parma-style anolini

✤ Reserve the beef. Strain the cooking liquid into a bowl. Discard the solids. Add the bread crumbs, cheese, nutmeg, and eggs to the cooking liquid. Add more cheese, if necessary, to make a soft, compact texture.

✤ For the pasta, place the flour in a mound on a work surface and make a well in the center. Add the eggs, olive oil, and salt. Knead to make a dough, then roll out into a very thin sheet. Cut into 2-inch (5-cm) diameter circles, then place ½ teaspoon of the filling in the center of each circle. Fold the pasta over the filling and press the edges together to seal.

✤ Bring the reserved homemade stock to a boil in a large saucepan and cook the anolini for 5–7 minutes, until they rise to the surface. Drain, reserving the stock. Serve immediately with the reserved stock and some shredded Parmesan cheese as a side dish, if desired. The capon, beef brisket, and beef steak can be served separately or kept for another use.

recipe hint

Capons are male chickens that are castrated when young and then fattened. Although they grow to be about twice the size of other young chickens, their flesh remains tender and succulent.

tagliatelle
with prosciutto
and radicchio

serves 4

1 lb (500 g) tagliatelle

7 tablespoons (3½ oz/105 g) butter, chopped

2 tablespoons olive oil

6½ oz (200 g) prosciutto

⅓ cup (½ oz/15 g) finely shredded fresh basil

8 radicchio leaves, washed and finely shredded

1 cup (4 oz/125 g) grated Parmesan cheese

ground black pepper

shavings of Parmesan cheese, to serve

❖ In a large saucepan of boiling salted water cook the pasta until al dente. Drain well, return to the pan and add the butter. Cover to keep warm.

❖ Meanwhile, heat the olive oil in a frying pan and fry the prosciutto until it is crisp. Drain on paper towels and then crumble into pieces.

❖ In a large bowl combine the basil, radicchio, grated Parmesan, pepper, and half of the prosciutto.

❖ Add the pasta to the bowl and toss quickly and thoroughly to combine. Serve topped with the Parmesan shavings and the remaining prosciutto.

farfalle
with creamy bacon and leek sauce

serves 4–6

Leeks have a subtle, delicate flavor that is both milder and sweeter than that of onions. The white part of the leek is the most tender and delicious. Before using, trim the green tops, then wash the leeks thoroughly as dirt can become trapped between the leaves.

8 oz (250 g) bacon

¼ cup (2 oz/60 g) butter

2 cloves garlic, finely chopped

1½ lb (750 g) baby leeks, washed, trimmed, and thinly sliced

1 cup (8 fl oz/250 ml) light (single) cream

½ cup (4 fl oz/125 ml) dry white wine

⅓ cup (2½ fl oz/80 ml) sour cream

1 cup (4 oz/125 g) grated Parmesan cheese

ground black pepper

¾ cup (3 oz/90 g) walnuts, roughly chopped

1 lb (500 g) farfalle (bow-tie pasta)

❖ Trim any excess fat and cut the bacon into large dice. Cook in a small frying pan, stirring, until the bacon is crisp. Set aside on paper towels to drain.

❖ Heat 3 tablespoons of the butter in a large frying pan and add the garlic and leeks. Cook gently over low heat, stirring often, until the leeks are very soft. Add the cream, wine, sour cream, and cheese and stir until the mixture is hot and slightly thickened; do not allow to boil. Stir in the bacon and pepper, to taste.

❖ Melt the remaining butter in a small saucepan. Add the walnuts and toss until lightly toasted.

❖ Meanwhile, in a large saucepan of boiling salted water cook the pasta until al dente; drain. Add the sauce and toss to combine. Serve immediately, sprinkled with the toasted walnuts.

recipe variations

You can replace the bacon with prosciutto, pancetta, or ham, if you prefer. Any shaped pasta may be used in this recipe, such as shell pasta, fusilli (spiral pasta), or elbow macaroni.

pumpkin and bacon
rigatoni

serves 4–6

3 cups (10 oz/315 g) chopped pumpkin flesh

1 lb (500 g) rigatoni

6½ oz (200 g) bacon, diced

1 clove garlic, finely chopped

½ cup (4 fl oz/125 ml) heavy (double) cream

1 tablespoon finely chopped fresh parsley

ground pepper

1 cup (4 oz/125 g) grated Parmesan cheese

❖ Steam the pumpkin until it is soft, then gently mash.

❖ In a large saucepan of boiling salted water cook the pasta until al dente.

❖ Meanwhile, in a small frying pan cook the bacon and garlic, stirring often, until the bacon is crisp.

❖ Place the mashed pumpkin in a saucepan and gradually stir in the cream. Stir in the bacon mixture and parsley, and gently heat the sauce. Season with pepper, to taste.

❖ Drain the pasta and return to the pan. Stir in the cheese. Add the sauce, toss to combine, and serve.

penne
with chile chard

serves 4

1 lb (500 g) penne

¼ cup (2 fl oz/60 ml) olive oil

1 clove garlic, finely chopped

*1 red (Spanish) onion,
finely chopped*

*1 small fresh red chile, seeded
and finely chopped*

*3½ oz (105 g) coppacolla or
smoked bacon, diced*

*8 stalks Swiss chard (silverbeet),
washed, hard stalk discarded,
leaves shredded*

salt and ground black pepper

*½ cup (2 oz/60 g) grated
Parmesan cheese*

❖ In a large saucepan of boiling salted water cook the pasta until al dente.

❖ Meanwhile, heat the olive oil in a frying pan and cook the garlic, onion, chile, and coppacolla or bacon, stirring often, for 2 minutes. Add the chard and stir until it just wilts. Season to taste with salt and pepper.

❖ Drain the pasta and return to the saucepan. Stir in the cheese. Add the chard mixture and stir well to combine. Serve immediately.

asparagus and ham
lasagna rolls

serves 4

This makes an excellent luncheon dish served with a green salad. If your béchamel sauce becomes lumpy, simply remove it from the heat and whisk vigorously until smooth.

fresh pasta sheets (about 1 lb/500 g total weight), cut into 8 equal squares

13 oz (410 g) asparagus

BECHAMEL SAUCE

7 tablespoons (3½ oz/105 g) butter

3 tablespoons all-purpose (plain) flour

1½ cups (12 fl oz/375 ml) milk

½ cup (4 fl oz/125 ml) dry white wine

½ cup (4 fl oz/125 ml) light (single) cream

1½ (6 oz/185 g) grated Parmesan cheese

8 slices (13 oz/410 g) ham

❖ In a large saucepan of boiling salted water cook the pasta squares, 1 or 2 at a time, for 2–3 minutes, or until they are just al dente. Transfer to kitchen towels to drain.

❖ Cook the asparagus in boiling water until just tender. Drain and refresh under cold water.

❖ For the béchamel sauce, melt the butter in a saucepan. Add the flour and stir to form a paste. Cook gently for 1–2 minutes. Remove the pan from the heat and gradually stir in the milk, then the wine. Return the pan to the heat and cook, stirring constantly, until the mixture boils and thickens. Stir in the cream and heat through without boiling. Cover and set aside.

❖ Preheat an oven to 350°F (180°C/Gas Mark 4).

❖ Spread 1 tablespoon of béchamel sauce over each pasta square, then sprinkle each with about 1 tablespoon of cheese. Top each pasta square with a slice of ham and 3–4 spears of asparagus. Roll up the sheets and secure with a toothpick, if necessary. Place the rolls side by side in a greased ceramic baking dish. Pour the remaining béchamel sauce over the top, ensuring that each roll is well coated. Sprinkle with the remaining cheese.

❖ Bake, uncovered, for about 30 minutes, or until the top is golden and bubbling.

stuffed pasta shells
in tomato sauce

serves 6

Giant pasta shells are perfect
for filling and then baking.
Experiment with different
fillings, using vegetables,
meat, or seafood as a base,
to create a quick, easy meal
the whole family will enjoy.

TOMATO SAUCE

3 tablespoons olive oil

2 onions, chopped

2 cloves garlic, chopped

*1 can (13 oz/425 g) peeled
Italian-style tomatoes*

2–3 bay leaves

1 tablespoon tomato paste

FILLING

3 cups (1½ lb/750 g) ricotta cheese

1 cup (1 oz/30 g) shredded fresh basil

1 egg, beaten lightly

5 oz (155 g) spicy salami, sliced and cut into julienne strips

salt and pepper

24 giant pasta shells, cooked in boiling salted water until al dente

WHITE WINE SAUCE

2 tablespoons butter

2 tablespoons all-purpose (plain) flour

1 cup (8 fl oz/250 ml) milk

1/2 cup (4 fl oz/125 ml) dry white wine

6 1/2 oz (200 g) mozzarella cheese, thinly sliced

1/2 cup (2 oz/60 g) grated Parmesan cheese

❖ For the tomato sauce, heat the oil in a large saucepan. Add the onions and garlic and cook, stirring often, until the onion is soft. Stir in the undrained tomatoes, bay leaves, and tomato paste. Bring to a boil, then reduce heat to low and simmer for 20–30 minutes, until reduced and thickened.

❖ Meanwhile, for the filling, place the ricotta, basil, egg, salami, salt, and pepper in a bowl and mix until well combined.

❖ Preheat an oven to 350°F (180°C/Gas Mark 4). Use a teaspoon to fill the pasta shells with the filling.

❖ For the white wine sauce, melt the butter in a saucepan. Add the flour and stir to form a paste. Cook gently for 1–2 minutes. Remove the pan from the heat and gradually stir in the milk, then the wine. Return the pan to the heat and cook, stirring constantly,

stuffed pasta shells in tomato sauce

until the mixture boils and thickens. Reduce the heat and cook gently for 1–2 minutes.

❖ Remove the bay leaves from the tomato sauce. Pour the sauce into a shallow 8-cup (2-qt/2-l) ovenproof dish. Arrange the stuffed pasta shells in the middle of the dish. Pour over half of the white wine sauce. Top the pasta shells with the mozzarella and pour over the remaining white wine sauce. Sprinkle with Parmesan.

❖ Bake for 20–25 minutes, or until the top is golden. Place briefly under a hot broiler (griller) to brown the top further, if desired. Serve immediately.

recipe hint

Ricotta is a fresh (or unripened) cheese that is made from sheep's-milk whey or cow's-milk whey, or even a combination of whey and milk. It is white, with a crumbly texture and a creamy, delicate flavor.

rigatoni
with mushrooms

serves 6

1¼ lb (625 g) ripe tomatoes

¼ cup (2 fl oz/60 ml) extra
virgin olive oil

2 cloves garlic, crushed

6 oz (185 g) pancetta, chopped

10 oz (315 g) fresh porcini
mushrooms, champignons, or
button mushrooms, sliced

⅓ cup (2½ fl oz/80 ml) dry
white wine

salt and ground pepper

1¼ lb (625 g) rigatoni

1 tablespoon chopped
fresh parsley

❖ Immerse the tomatoes in boiling water for about
30 seconds. Drain, then peel and chop.

❖ In a large frying pan, heat the oil and gently cook
the garlic until translucent. Add the pancetta and
mushrooms and stir over medium heat for 5 minutes.
Stir in the wine. Add the tomatoes and season to taste
with salt and pepper. Cook over low heat, stirring
occasionally, for 30 minutes, or until most of the liquid
has evaporated.

❖ Meanwhile, in a large saucepan of boiling salted
water cook the pasta until al dente. Drain well.

❖ Place the pasta in a serving dish and carefully mix in
half of the mushroom sauce. Top with the remaining
sauce, and serve sprinkled with parsley.

ham and ricotta cannelloni

serves 4

Cannelloni is a true comfort food. The large tubes of pasta are stuffed with a savory filling, topped with a tomato or cheese sauce and baked until the pasta is tender and the filling is heated through. Serve with a dressed green salad and crusty Italian bread.

SAUCE

2 tablespoons olive oil

1 large onion, finely chopped

2 cloves garlic, crushed

1 can (28 oz/880 g) peeled plum (Roma) tomatoes

1½ tablespoons tomato paste

2 tablespoons chopped fresh basil leaves

salt and ground pepper

1 lb (500 g) cannelloni tubes

1 cup (8 oz/250 g) ricotta cheese

2 thick slices ham, diced

1 egg

salt and ground pepper

3½ oz (105 g) grated Parmesan cheese

❖ For the sauce, heat the oil in a saucepan and cook the onion and garlic, stirring often, until the onion is soft. Stir in the undrained tomatoes, tomato paste, basil, salt, and pepper. Bring to a boil, then reduce heat and simmer for 30 minutes, or until smooth and thick.

❖ Meanwhile, if cannelloni tubes are not precooked, cook them in boiling salted water until al dente; drain.

❖ Preheat an oven to 350°F (180°C/Gas Mark 4).

❖ Place the ricotta, ham, egg, salt, and pepper in a bowl and mix until well combined.

❖ Use a teaspoon to carefully stuff the filling into the cannelloni tubes. Place the filled tubes in a single layer in a well-greased, shallow baking dish. Pour over the sauce and ensure that all the tubes are covered. Sprinkle with cheese. Bake for 30 minutes, or until the top is nicely browned.

recipe variations

There are many filling variations for cannelloni. In this recipe, you can substitute bacon, pancetta or prosciutto for the ham, if desired. The Parmesan can be replaced with fontina, mozzarella, or Cheddar cheese.

baked pasta
with eggplant

serves 6

The eggplant can be fried in advance. Store in the refrigerator, layered with plastic wrap to prevent the slices sticking together. The tomato sauce can be made up to 3 days in advance and kept in the refrigerator. Or it can be cooked further ahead and frozen.

3 medium eggplants (aubergines)

salt

2 cups (16 fl oz/500 ml) olive oil

2 lb (1 kg) very ripe tomatoes, chopped

3 cloves garlic

1/2 teaspoon ground black pepper

1/2 teaspoon sugar

2 tablespoons finely chopped fresh parsley

1 tablespoon chopped fresh basil

1 lb (500 g) macaroni

4 oz (125 g) spicy salami, diced

4 oz (125 g) mozzarella cheese, diced

2/3 cup (2 2/3 oz/80 g) finely grated pecorino romano or Parmesan cheese

2–3 hard-boiled eggs, peeled and sliced

❖ Preheat an oven to 375°F (190°C/Gas Mark 5).

❖ Cut the eggplants into ¼-inch (6-mm) slices. Sprinkle the slices on both sides with salt and place them in a colander to drain for 15 minutes to rid them of their bitter juices. Wash the slices under cold water, then place on paper towels to dry.

❖ Meanwhile, heat 3 tablespoons of the oil in a frying pan. Cook the tomatoes and garlic until soft and pulpy. Stir in ¾ teaspoon of salt, the pepper, sugar, and herbs and cook for 5 minutes.

❖ Bring a large saucepan of salted water to the boil. Add the pasta and 1 tablespoon of the oil and cook until the pasta is almost tender. Drain well and place in a large mixing bowl. Add the salami, mozzarella, pecorino romano or Parmesan, and the tomato mixture and stir to combine. Set aside.

❖ Lightly grease a pie dish with olive oil. Heat the remaining oil in a frying pan. Add the eggplant and cook until lightly colored and softened. Arrange the eggplant slices, overlapping each other, to completely line the pie dish. Place the sliced eggs over the eggplant, then add the pasta mixture. Press any remaining eggplant over the top. Bake for 30 minutes, then set aside for 7 minutes before turning onto a serving dish. Cut into wedges and serve with extra grated pecorino romano or Parmesan cheese and a green salad, if desired.

spaghetti
with braised pork ribs

serves 6

2½ lb (1.25 kg) meaty pork spareribs

2 tablespoons olive or vegetable oil

1 large onion, chopped

3 cloves garlic, chopped

1 can (14 oz/440 g) crushed tomatoes

1½ cups (12 fl oz/375 ml) water

1 cinnamon stick

1 bay leaf

1 clove

½–1 teaspoon paprika

salt and ground black pepper

3 tablespoons finely chopped fresh parsley

1½ lb (750 g) spaghetti

⅓ cup (¾ oz/20 g) pitted black olives

finely grated Parmesan cheese (optional)

❖ Preheat an oven to 350°F (180°C/Gas Mark 4).

❖ Place the spareribs in a casserole. In a saucepan heat the oil and cook the onion and garlic, stirring often, until softened. Stir in the tomatoes and water and bring to a boil. Pour over the spareribs and add the cinnamon stick, bay leaf, and clove. Cover and bake for 2 hours, or until the spareribs are very tender.

❖ Remove the spareribs and cut the meat into small cubes. Transfer the sauce to a saucepan and stir in the paprika, salt, pepper, and half of the parsley. Boil until the sauce reduces to about 3 cups (24 fl oz/750 ml). Stir in the meat. Remove and discard the cinnamon stick, bay leaf, and clove.

❖ Meanwhile, in a large saucepan of boiling salted water cook the pasta until al dente. Drain, then add the sauce and toss to combine. Serve garnished with the olives, cheese (if using), and remaining parsley.

recipe hint

Spareribs are narrow, fatty cuts of meat that are taken from the upper part of the pork belly with the lower portion of the ribs attached.

spaghetti
with meatballs

serves 6

The simplicity and goodness
of this Italian-American dish
make it a popular family
favorite. You can make the
meatballs as small or large
as you like. Simply adjust
the frying time as necessary.

¼ cup (2 fl oz/60 ml) olive oil

8 green (spring) onions, including the tender
green tops, finely chopped

2 cloves garlic, finely chopped

½ teaspoon dried thyme, crumbled

1 teaspoon dried basil, crumbled

1 wedge (3 oz/90 g) Parmesan cheese

2 lb (1 kg) ground (minced) lean beef

salt and ground black pepper

1 egg, beaten lightly

½ cup (2 oz/60 g) fine dried bread crumbs

2 tablespoons finely chopped fresh parsley

1¼ lb (625 g) spaghetti

6 cups (48 fl oz/1.5 l) Herb and
Tomato Sauce (page 101)

❖ In a small frying pan over medium-low heat warm 2 tablespoons of the olive oil. Add the green onions and cook, stirring often, until they are almost translucent, 3–4 minutes. Add the garlic and stir for 1 minute. Stir in the thyme and half of the basil and cook for 1 minute. Set the mixture aside to cool.

❖ Grate enough of the cheese to measure ¼ cup (1 oz/30 g); set aside. Use a vegetable peeler to shave the remaining cheese into thin slices; set aside to use as a garnish.

❖ In a large bowl, combine the beef and green onion mixture. Use your hands to mix the ingredients together until they are thoroughly combined. Add ½ teaspoon salt, ¼ teaspoon pepper, the grated cheese, egg, bread crumbs, and parsley. Mix until combined. Cover and refrigerate for 30–40 minutes to make the mixture easier to handle.

❖ Shape the chilled meat mixture into 1½-inch (4-cm) balls. Heat the remaining olive oil in a large frying pan over medium heat. Add the meatballs to the pan in a single layer, making sure that they are not touching (cook in batches, if necessary). Cook, turning to brown evenly on all sides, for about 15 minutes. Cover the pan, then reduce the heat to low and continue cooking until the meatballs are cooked through, about 8 minutes longer. Use a slotted spoon to transfer the meatballs to paper towels to drain.

❖ In a large saucepan of boiling salted water cook the pasta until al dente; drain. Return to the pan and cover to keep warm.

spaghetti with meatballs

❖ Meanwhile, in a large saucepan over medium heat combine the tomato sauce and remaining basil. Bring the mixture to a simmer, then add the meatballs. Cover and simmer until the meatballs have taken on the flavor of the sauce, about 5–7 minutes.

❖ Transfer the spaghetti to a large serving platter or individual pasta bowls. Ladle the meatballs and sauce over the top and then sprinkle with the reserved shaved cheese. Serve immediately.

recipe **variation**

The meatball mixture in this recipe can also be made into hamburger patties, if desired. Simply shape into patties and cook under a hot broiler (griller) or barbecue until browned on both sides and cooked through. Serve on toasted hamburger buns with mustard, tomato ketchup, cheese, lettuce, and tomato.

classic cannelloni

serves 4

FILLING

2 teaspoons sunflower, safflower,
or canola oil

2 tablespoons finely chopped yellow onion

4 oz (125 g) ground (minced) pork
shoulder or butt, or ground veal

4 oz (125 g) mortadella, ground (minced)

2 oz (60 g) prosciutto, ground (minced)

2 cups (1 lb/500 g) ricotta cheese

¾ cup (3 oz/90 g) grated Parmesan cheese

salt and ground white pepper

pinch of grated nutmeg

5 oz (155 g) purchased thin
fresh pasta sheets

WHITE SAUCE

¼ cup (2 oz/60 g) sweet (unsalted) butter

⅓ cup (1½ oz/45 g) all-purpose (plain) flour

3 cups (24 fl oz/750 ml) milk,
heated almost to a boil

salt and ground white pepper

pinch of grated nutmeg

iced water, as needed

½ cup (2 oz/60 g) grated Parmesan cheese

classic cannelloni

◈ For the filling, heat the oil in a small frying pan over medium heat. Add the onion and cook, stirring, until it is almost translucent, about 3 minutes. Add the pork or veal and cook, stirring occasionally, for 5 minutes; do not allow to brown. Transfer to a colander to drain and cool.

◈ In a bowl combine the cooled meat mixture, mortadella, prosciutto, ricotta, and Parmesan. Season to taste with salt and pepper, and add the nutmeg. Set aside.

◈ Cut the pasta sheets into eight 4½-inch (11.5-cm) squares. Set aside.

◈ For the white sauce, melt the butter in a saucepan over low heat. Whisk in the flour, then gradually add the hot milk, whisking constantly. Simmer, whisking constantly, until the mixture boils and thickens, about 5 minutes. Remove from the heat, season to taste with salt and pepper, and add the nutmeg.

◈ In a large saucepan of boiling salted water cook the pasta until almost al dente, about 2 minutes. Drain, then plunge into iced water to stop the cooking process. Drain again and lay flat in a single layer on kitchen towels to dry briefly.

◈ Preheat an oven to 450°F (220°C/Gas Mark 6). Spread 1 cup (8 fl oz/250 ml) of the white sauce over the base of a 9- x 12-inch (23- x 30-cm) baking dish. Shape about ⅓ cup (2 oz/60 g) of the filling into a log. Place on the center of a pasta square and roll the pasta tightly around the filling. Repeat with the remaining filling and pasta squares. Place the rolls, seam-side down,

classic cannelloni

in a single layer in the dish. Spread the remaining white sauce over the rolls and sprinkle evenly with the cheese.

❖ Place in the center of the oven and reduce the temperature to 400°F (200°C/Gas Mark 5). Bake until the top is bubbling and golden brown, 30–35 minutes. Remove the cannelloni from the oven and set aside for 5 minutes before serving.

recipe variations

The meat-and-ricotta filling used to stuff the cannelloni tubes can also be used to stuff ravioli or tortellini. The white sauce may be replaced by Herb and Tomato Sauce (page 101), if desired.

serves 4

SPINACH PASTA

3¼ cups (13 oz/410 g)
all-purpose (plain) flour

9 eggs

3½ oz (105 g) cooked,
chopped spinach, excess
water squeezed out

SAUCE

3½ oz (105 g) butter

3½ oz (105 g) prosciutto,
cut into thin strips

3½ oz (105 g) shelled fresh
green peas

1 cup (1 oz/30 g) mixed
chopped fresh herbs, such as
basil, mint, marjoram,
chicory, thyme, and rosemary

¾ cup (3 oz/90 g) grated
Parmesan cheese

❖ For the pasta, place the flour in a large mixing bowl and make a well in the center. Add the eggs and mix to form a dough. Divide the dough into 2 portions. Add the spinach to 1 portion and work it in. Roll out each portion into a thin sheet.

❖ Use a fluted pastry wheel to cut each pasta sheet into 1½- x ¾-inch (4- x 2-cm) rectangles. Gently pinch the middle of each rectangle to form a butterfly shape.

❖ For the sauce, in a large frying pan melt half of the butter. Add the prosciutto and cook, stirring, until it is browned. Stir in the peas and herbs and cook until the peas are tender.

❖ Meanwhile, cook the pasta in a large saucepan of boiling salted water until al dente; drain. Add the pasta and remaining butter to the frying pan and toss with the sauce to combine. Serve immediately, sprinkled with the cheese.

butterfly pasta
with ham, peas, and herbs

stuffed pasta rolls

serves 3–4

1 portion Spinach Pasta (page 305)

FILLING

½ cup (½ oz/15 g) fresh chives

½ cup (½ oz/15 g) fresh parsley

1–2 small cloves garlic

1 cup (8 oz/250 g) cream cheese

½ cup (4 oz/125 g) cottage cheese

5 oz (155 g) thinly sliced
prosciutto or ham

4 oz (125 g) drained, finely chopped,
oil-packed sun-dried tomatoes

¼ cup (2 fl oz/60 ml) chicken stock,
white wine, or water

SAUCE

3 tablespoons butter

2 cups (6 oz/185 g) sliced fresh
mushrooms

2 cloves garlic, finely chopped

3 tablespoons all-purpose
(plain) flour

¼ teaspoon salt

¼ teaspoon ground white pepper

1 cup (8 fl oz/250 ml) chicken stock

1 cup (8 fl oz/250 ml) light (single)
cream or milk

½ teaspoon finely
shredded lemon
zest (rind)

1 tablespoon
fresh lemon juice

2 tablespoons
grated Parmesan cheese

❖ Prepare the pasta as directed, but divide dough in half instead of quarters. Roll out each half to a 12- x 6-inch (30- x 15-cm) rectangle. Cook 1 pasta sheet in plenty of boiling salted water until al dente, about 3 minutes. Use a slotted spoon to transfer to a colander. Rinse under cold water, then drain well. Carefully transfer the pasta sheet to a damp kitchen towel. Repeat with the remaining pasta sheet.

❖ Meanwhile, for the filling, use a food processor or blender to process the chives, parsley, garlic, cream cheese, and cottage cheese until almost smooth.

❖ Preheat an oven to 375°F (190°C/Gas Mark 4). Spread the cheese mixture over the pasta sheets, leaving a ¼-inch (6-mm) border. Layer the prosciutto or ham and sun-dried tomatoes on top. Roll up, starting from a short side. (If desired, cover pasta rolls and chill for up to 24 hours.) Trim uneven edges and cut each roll into 6 slices. Place slices, cut-side down, in an 8-cup (2-qt/2-l) rectangular baking dish. Pour the stock, wine, or water over and around the pasta rolls. Bake, covered, for 20 minutes, or until heated through.

❖ Meanwhile, for the sauce, melt the butter in a medium saucepan. Add mushrooms and garlic and cook until tender. Stir in flour, salt, and pepper. Add chicken stock and cream or milk. Cook, stirring, until mixture boils and thickens. Boil, stirring, for 1 minute. Remove from heat and stir in lemon zest and juice. To serve, spoon sauce onto plates and arrange hot pasta rolls on top. Sprinkle with parmesan and serve at once.

187

ham tortellini
with cheese sauce

serves 4–6

2 portions Spinach Pasta (page 305)

FILLING

2 teaspoons butter

2 tablespoons finely chopped celery

2 tablespoons finely chopped onion

4 oz (125 g) ground (minced) ham

1 egg yolk, beaten

SAUCE

2 tablespoons butter

4 teaspoons all-purpose (plain) flour

1½ cups (12 fl oz/375 ml) milk

½ cup (2 oz/60 g) shredded Swiss cheese

2 tablespoons chopped fresh parsley

❖ Prepare pasta as directed. With a 1¼-inch (3-cm) cutter, cut 96 circles. Cover and set aside.

❖ For the filling, melt the butter in a small saucepan. Add celery and onion and cook, stirring occasionally, until tender, about 5 minutes. Remove from heat and stir in the ham and egg yolk. Place about ¼ teaspoon of filling in the center of a pasta circle. Fold the circle in half and press the edges together. Place a finger against the fold and bring the corners together, pressing to seal. Repeat with remaining pasta circles and filling. Set aside for 10 minutes.

❖ Preheat an oven to 300°F (150°C/Gas Mark 2). In a large saucepan of boiling salted water cook half of the tortellini until al dente, 6–8 minutes. Use a slotted spoon to transfer to a large greased casserole. Repeat with the remaining tortellini. Cover the casserole and place in the oven while you make the sauce.

❖ For the sauce, melt the butter in a small saucepan. Stir in flour. Add milk and cook, stirring, until mixture boils and thickens. Boil, stirring, for 1 minute. Stir in the cheese and parsley.

❖ Serve the sauce spooned over the hot tortellini.

fettuccine
with asparagus, ham, and cheese

serves 4

1 lb (500 g) fresh fettuccine

12 asparagus spears

4 oz (125 g) ham or prosciutto, diced

¾ cup (3 oz/90 g) grated pecorino romano cheese

2 tablespoons butter

1½ teaspoons finely chopped fresh parsley

❖ In a large saucepan of boiling salted water cook the pasta until al dente, 1–2 minutes. Drain.

❖ Meanwhile, in a separate saucepan, cook the asparagus in simmering lightly salted water until it is tender enough to be easily pierced with a fork, 2–3 minutes. Drain; cut into ¾-inch (2-cm) pieces.

❖ Place the hot pasta in a bowl and add the asparagus, ham or prosciutto, half the cheese, and the butter; toss to combine. Serve sprinkled with the remaining cheese and the parsley.

lasagne bolognese

serves 4

1 portion Spinach Pasta (pages 304–305)
or 1 lb (500 g) purchased lasagna noodles

1 quantity White Sauce (pages 181–182)

8 oz (250 g) Parmesan cheese, grated

salt and ground pepper

BOLOGNESE SAUCE

3 tablespoons sunflower or canola oil

⅓ cup (2 oz/60 g) diced carrot

⅓ cup (2 oz/60 g) diced celery

⅓ cup (2 oz/60 g) diced yellow onion

6 oz (185 g) pancetta, coarsely ground
(minced) or finely chopped

12 oz (375 g) coarsely ground (minced)
or finely chopped pork butt or shoulder

6 oz (185 g) coarsely ground (minced)
or finely chopped veal

2 cans (28 oz/880 g each) plum (Roma)
tomatoes, drained and chopped,
plus juice from 1 can

salt and ground pepper

grated nutmeg

❖ Prepare spinach pasta as directed, if using, then roll out the dough until ¹⁄₁₆ inch (2 mm) thick. Cover with a damp kitchen towel and set aside.

❖ To make the sauce, heat the oil in a large saucepan over low heat. Add the carrot and celery and cook until the edges of the celery are translucent, about 5 minutes. Add the onion and cook until almost translucent, about 5 minutes. Add the pancetta and cook, stirring occasionally, for 10 minutes. Add the pork and veal and cook, stirring occasionally, until cooked but not browned, about 15 minutes. Add the tomatoes and juice and simmer, uncovered, stirring occasionally, until very thick, 2–2½ hours. Season to taste with salt, pepper, and nutmeg.

❖ Cut the fresh pasta, if using, into sixteen 4- x 10-inch (10- x 25-cm) strips. Prepare the white sauce and set aside.

lasagna bolognese

❖ In a large saucepan of boiling salted water cook the pasta, stirring occasionally, until not quite al dente (about 2 minutes for fresh pasta and 6 minutes for dried). Drain and then plunge the pasta into iced water to halt the cooking process. Drain again and lay flat in a single layer on kitchen towels to dry briefly.

❖ Preheat an oven to 450°F (220°C/Gas Mark 6). Select a 9- x 12-inch (23- x 30-cm) baking dish. Spread ½ cup (4 fl oz/125 ml) of the bolognese sauce over the base of the dish. Arrange a single layer of pasta on top, being careful not to overlap. Spread ⅓ cup (2½ fl oz/80 ml) of the white sauce over the top and then another ½–⅔ cup (4–5 fl oz/ 125–160 ml) bolognese sauce. Sprinkle with 3–4 tablespoons of the Parmesan cheese, then season with salt and pepper. Repeat layering the pasta, sauces, and cheese to make 7 layers in all. Arrange a final pasta layer on top, spread with the remaining white sauce, and sprinkle with the remaining cheese.

❖ Place in the center of the oven and reduce temperature to 400°F (200°C/Gas Mark 5). Bake until the lasagna is bubbling and golden brown, 35–45 minutes. Remove from the oven and set aside for 5 minutes before serving.

sausage & tomato sauce

makes 8 cups (32 fl oz/1 liter)

2 lb (1 kg) ripe plum (Roma) tomatoes or 30 oz (940 g) canned Italian-style tomatoes, cut up, drained

12 oz (375 g) Italian-style sausages (casings removed)

2½ oz (75 g) chopped onion

2 oz (60 g) finely chopped green bell pepper (capsicum)

2 cloves garlic, finely chopped

6 oz (185 g) tomato paste

½ teaspoon salt

½ teaspoon dried oregano, crushed

½ teaspoon dried basil, crushed

¼ teaspoon cayenne pepper

❖ Peel, seed, and chop the fresh tomatoes, if using.

❖ In a large saucepan cook the sausages, onion, bell pepper, and garlic, stirring, for 5 minutes, or until the sausage meat is browned. Drain off fat. Carefully stir in the fresh or drained canned tomatoes, tomato paste, salt, oregano, basil, and cayenne pepper. Bring to a boil. Reduce heat, cover, and simmer for 30 minutes. Uncover and simmer, stirring occasionally, for 10–15 minutes, or until the sauce has thickened to the desired consistency.

❖ Serve the sauce spooned over the hot cooked pasta of your choice.

orecchiette with fennel

serves 2–3

4 oz (125 g) orecchiette

1 fennel bulb

3 tablespoons butter

3–4 oz (90–125 g) fresh shiitake mushrooms, stems removed, sliced

2½ oz (75 g) finely chopped onion

2 oz (60 g) prosciutto, cut into strips

½ cup (¾ oz/20 g) chopped fresh parsley

½ cup (4 fl oz/125 ml) heavy (double) cream

½ cup (2 oz/60 g) grated Parmesan cheese

¼ cup (2 fl oz/60 ml) chicken stock

1 egg, beaten

1 tablespoon anise-flavored liqueur

½ teaspoon aniseeds

❖ In a large saucepan of boiling salted water cook the pasta until al dente; drain.

❖ Meanwhile, clean, trim, and slice the fennel bulb. Melt the butter in a large frying pan over medium-high heat and cook the fennel, stirring, for 3 minutes. Add the mushrooms and onion and cook, stirring, for 5 minutes more. Add the prosciutto and parsley and stir to combine.

❖ In a small mixing bowl combine the cream, cheese, stock, egg, liqueur, and aniseeds. Add to the frying pan and stir well to combine. Cook, stirring, until the cheese melts and the sauce thickens slightly. Add the hot cooked pasta and toss to combine. Serve immediately.

pappardelle
with venison ragû

serves 4

MARINADE

1 teaspoon fresh rosemary leaves

4 fresh sage leaves

2 bay leaves

1 cinnamon stick

1 teaspoon juniper berries

⅛ teaspoon cloves

1 lb (500 g) venison shoulder, cut into 1-inch (2.5-cm) cubes

1 celery stalk, quartered

1 carrot, peeled and quartered

1 yellow onion, quartered

1½ cups (12 fl oz/375 ml) red wine

RAGÛ

2 tablespoons butter

1 teaspoon fresh rosemary leaves

1 fresh sage leaf

1 bay leaf

1 cinnamon stick

¼ cup (1⅓ oz/40 g) each of diced yellow onion, carrot, and celery

1 teaspoon finely chopped garlic

1 cup (6 oz/185 g) peeled and chopped plum (Roma) tomatoes

½ cup (4 fl oz/125 ml) red wine

2 tablespoons dry Marsala wine

2½ cups (20 fl oz/625 ml) beef stock

4 oz (250 g) pappardelle

2 tablespoons butter, melted

pappardelle with venison ragû

❖ For the marinade, place the rosemary, sage, bay leaves, cinnamon stick, juniper berries, and cloves on a square of cheesecloth (muslin). Bring the corners together and tie with kitchen string to secure. In a shallow nonaluminum bowl, combine the venison, celery, carrot, onion, wine, and cheesecloth bag. Cover and refrigerate overnight.

❖ Remove the venison from the marinade; discard the marinade and cheesecloth bag.

❖ For the ragû, melt 1 tablespoon of the butter in a large saucepan over high heat. Add the venison and cook until it is browned on all sides, about 10 minutes. Transfer the venison to a plate and set aside. Place the rosemary, sage, bay leaf, and cinnamon stick on another square of cheesecloth and tie with kitchen string to secure. Melt the remaining 1 tablespoon butter in the same saucepan over medium heat. Add the onion, carrot, and celery and cook, stirring often, until the onion and celery are translucent, about 5 minutes. Add the garlic, cheesecloth bag, and tomatoes and cook, stirring, for 2 minutes. Stir in the venison and red wine and cook for 2 minutes.

❖ Add the Marsala to the pan and cook, stirring, for 1 minute longer. Stir in the stock and bring to a boil over high heat. Reduce the heat to low and simmer, uncovered, until the venison is tender and the liquid has reduced to about 2 cups (16 fl oz/500 ml), about 45–55 minutes.

pappardelle with venison ragû

❖ Use a slotted spoon to transfer the venison to a plate and set aside. Discard the cheesecloth bag. Ladle the vegetable mixture into a food processor and process until puréed. Return to the pan and bring to a simmer over low heat. Simmer for 5 minutes. Stir in the venison and continue to simmer until the sauce is thick, about 15 minutes.

❖ Meanwhile, in a large saucepan of boiling salted water cook the pasta until al dente. Drain the pasta and return to the pan.

❖ Add the melted butter to the pasta and toss well. Add the venison ragû and toss to combine. Serve immediately.

spaghetti bolognese

serves 6

Prepare the sauce several hours in advance, if possible, to allow time for the flavors to develop. The sauce can be prepared up to several days in advance and stored in an airtight container in the refrigerator. Or, you can freeze the sauce in airtight containers. Remove from the freezer 2–3 hours before using to allow time to thaw.

3 tablespoons olive oil

8 oz (250 g) ground (minced) lean beef

8 oz (250 g) ground (minced) lean veal

4 oz (125 g) bacon, finely chopped

1 large onion, finely chopped

2–3 cloves garlic, finely chopped

2 large chicken livers, finely chopped

1 bay leaf

1 tablespoon finely chopped fresh parsley, plus extra for garnish

1½ lb (750 g) ripe tomatoes

3 tablespoons tomato paste

¾ teaspoon sugar

salt and ground pepper

1 teaspoon chopped fresh basil

1½ lb (750 g) spaghetti

finely grated Parmesan cheese, to serve

✥ Heat the olive oil in a large saucepan over medium heat. Add the beef and veal and cook, stirring to break up any lumps, until well browned. In a small frying pan, cook the bacon until well browned, then use a slotted spoon to add it to the saucepan. Cook the onion in the bacon fat until it is soft and golden. Add the garlic and chicken livers and cook until the livers change color. Add to the saucepan with the bay leaf and parsley and stir to combine.

✥ Immerse the tomatoes in boiling water for about 30 seconds to loosen their skins. Peel and then cut the tomatoes in half. Squeeze the seeds into a sieve over a bowl, so any liquid is reserved. Finely chop the tomatoes. Add to the meat mixture and cook, stirring occasionally, for 15 minutes. Stir in the tomato paste, sugar, salt, and pepper and simmer for about 40 minutes. If the sauce becomes dry, add the reserved juice from the tomatoes. Stir in the basil a few minutes before the sauce is done.

✥ Meanwhile, in a large saucepan of boiling salted water cook the pasta until al dente; drain. Divide among serving bowls, spoon the sauce over the top, and sprinkle with the cheese and extra parsley. Serve immediately.

sweet & sour
fettuccine

serves 2

If you decide to use spinach
or Swiss chard (silverbeet)
instead of kale, take note
that they cook in much
less time. Start by cooking
the pasta and then cook
the vegetables.

4 oz (125 g) dried fettuccine or linguine, or
8 oz (250 g) fresh fettuccine or linguine

6 oz (185 g) kale, spinach, or Swiss chard (silverbeet)

6 oz (185 g) yellow baby squash or zucchini
(courgettes), cut into ¼-inch (6-mm) thick slices

2 tablespoons olive oil

1 oz (30 g) pancetta or thickly sliced bacon,
finely chopped

½ cup (2 oz/60 g) chopped onion

1 tablespoon all-purpose (plain) flour

1 tablespoon sugar

½ teaspoon salt

⅛ teaspoon pepper

¾ cup (6 fl oz/185 ml) chicken stock

¼ cup (2 fl oz/60 ml) red wine vinegar

❖ In a large saucepan of boiling salted water cook the pasta until al dente (8–10 minutes for dried pasta, 1–2 minutes for fresh pasta). Drain and cover to keep warm.

❖ Wash the kale, spinach, or chard. Remove the center ribs, if necessary, and tear each leaf into bite-sized pieces. In a large saucepan bring 1 cup (8 fl oz/250 ml) water to a boil. Add the kale (if using) and simmer, covered, for 25 minutes. Add the squash, zucchini, and spinach or chard, if using, and cook for 3–5 minutes, until tender. Drain and keep warm.

❖ Meanwhile, if using pancetta, heat the oil in a large frying pan and cook the pancetta until browned. (If using bacon, omit the oil.) Add the onion and cook, stirring often, until it is tender. Stir in the flour, sugar, salt, and pepper. Stir in the stock and vinegar and cook, stirring, until the mixture boils and thickens. Simmer, stirring, for 2 minutes more. Stir in the cooked vegetables and mix well. Spoon over the hot cooked pasta and serve immediately.

stuffed peppers
with orzo

serves 4

Orzo, also known as risoni, is a type of pasta that is shaped like rice, and is often used in recipes as a substitute for rice. Here, it is cooked in the stuffing mixture, saving the step of cooking the pasta separately.

2 large red, yellow, and/or green bell peppers (capsicums)

12 oz (375 g) ground (minced) lamb, turkey, or pork

¼ cup (1 oz/30 g) chopped onion

8 oz (250 g) canned Italian-style tomatoes, chopped

2 oz (60 g) orzo (risoni)

1 tablespoon chopped fresh mint, basil, or oregano, or ½ teaspoon dried mint, basil, or oregano, crushed

½ teaspoon ground allspice

½ cup (4 fl oz/125 ml) water

salt and ground pepper

½ cup (2 oz/60 g) grated Parmesan cheese

❖ Preheat an oven to 375°F (190°C/Gas Mark 4). Halve the bell peppers lengthways and remove the stems, seeds, and membranes. Plunge into boiling water for 3 minutes. Remove, sprinkle the insides with salt, and invert onto paper towels to drain.

❖ In a frying pan over medium-high heat cook the meat and onion for 5 minutes, or until the meat is browned and onion is tender. Drain off the fat. Stir in the tomatoes, pasta, mint, basil, or oregano, allspice, water, salt, and pepper. Bring to a boil, then reduce the heat. Cover and simmer for 7 minutes, or until the pasta is al dente. Stir in half of the cheese.

❖ Place the bell peppers, cut-side up, in a 8-cup (2-qt/2-l) square baking dish. Use a spoon to fill the bell peppers with the meat mixture. Bake for 15 minutes, or until heated through. Sprinkle with the remaining cheese and set aside for 1–2 minutes before serving.

recipe hint

Allspice is also known as "pimiento" and "Jamaica pepper." The small berries are produced by a tropical tree mainly cultivated in Jamaica, and have the aroma of cinnamon, cloves, and nutmeg all at once. The berries can be used whole in preserves and chutneys, or, if ground, in baked goods, desserts, and savory dishes.

artichoke, lamb, and orzo avgolemono

serves 4–6

2 tablespoons olive oil

1 lb (500 g) boneless lean lamb, cut into ¾-inch (2-cm) cubes

1 cup (4 oz/125 g) chopped onion

1 clove garlic, finely chopped

¾ cup (6 fl oz/185 ml) white wine or chicken stock

1½ teaspoons chopped fresh oregano or ½ teaspoon dried oregano, crushed

1 teaspoon finely shredded lemon zest (rind)

salt and ground black pepper

6 fresh medium artichokes, tops trimmed, tough outer leaves removed, halved lengthwise, and blanched, or 9 oz (280 g) frozen artichoke hearts, thawed

8 oz (250 g) orzo (risoni)

1 egg, beaten lightly

2 tablespoons fresh lemon juice

1 tablespoon cornstarch (cornflour)

½ cup (4 fl oz/125 ml) warm chicken stock

2 tablespoons chopped fresh parsley (optional)

❖ Heat the oil in a large frying pan and cook half of the lamb until browned; transfer to a plate. Add the remaining lamb, the onion, and garlic to the pan and cook until the meat is browned and onion is tender. Drain off fat. Return all the meat to the pan. Stir in the wine or stock, oregano, lemon zest, salt, and pepper. Bring to a boil, then reduce the heat. Cover and simmer for 20 minutes. Stir in the artichokes and simmer for 10 minutes more, or until tender.

❖ Meanwhile, in a large saucepan of boiling salted water cook the pasta until al dente. Drain and return to the saucepan; cover to keep warm.

❖ In a small mixing bowl combine the egg, lemon juice, cornstarch, and warm chicken stock. Add to the lamb mixture and cook over medium heat, stirring, for 1 minute, or until the mixture boils. Boil, stirring, for 2 minutes. Spoon over the hot cooked pasta and serve immediately, sprinkled with parsley, if desired.

rigatoni
with sausages

serves 4

1 lb (500 g) Italian sausages

3 oz (90 g) fresh mushrooms

½ cup (2 oz/60 g)
chopped onion

13½ oz (425 g) bottled
Italian-style tomato sauce

½ cup (4 fl oz/125 ml) dry
white or red wine

2 tablespoons chopped
fresh parsley

1 teaspoon dried Italian
seasoning, crushed

salt and ground pepper

8 oz (250 g) rigatoni or penne

❖ Remove the casings from the sausages. Brush the mushrooms to remove any dirt, trim the stems and slice. In a large frying pan cook the sausage meat, mushrooms, and onion for 5 minutes, or until the sausage is browned and onion is tender. Drain off fat. Add the tomato sauce, wine, parsley, Italian seasoning, salt, and pepper. Bring to a boil, then reduce the heat. Cover and simmer for 30 minutes. Uncover and simmer for 10–15 minutes more, or to the desired consistency, stirring occasionally to prevent sticking.

❖ Meanwhile, in a large saucepan of boiling salted water cook the pasta until al dente. Drain, add the sauce and toss to combine. Serve immediately.

pasta
with peas and ham

serves 2

4 oz (125 g) conchiglie,
cavatelli, or other
shell-shaped pasta

2 tablespoons butter

1 oz (30 g) pancetta or bacon,
finely chopped

1½ oz (45 g) thinly sliced
green (spring) onions

5 oz (155 g) frozen small peas

1 tablespoon water

4 oz (125 g) mascarpone
cheese

salt and pepper

1–2 tablespoons milk (optional)

❖ In a large saucepan of boiling salted water cook the pasta until al dente; drain.

❖ Meanwhile, if using pancetta, melt the butter in a medium saucepan and cook the pancetta and green onions for 2 minutes, or until the onions are just tender. (If using bacon, omit the butter but cook with the onions as directed.) Add the peas and water, cover and simmer for 3 minutes. Stir in the mascarpone until melted. Season with salt and pepper, to taste. Add the hot cooked pasta and toss to coat. If the mixture is too thick, add a little milk. Serve immediately.

four seasons pasta pie

serves 4 as an appetizer

CRUST

5 oz (155 g) dried spaghetti or linguine or
10 oz (315 g) fresh linguine

1 egg, beaten lightly

¼ cup (1 oz/30 g) grated Parmesan cheese

1 tablespoon butter

CHEESE FILLING

1 egg, beaten lightly

1 cup (8 oz/250 g) ricotta cheese

pepper

TOPPING

1 teaspoon olive oil

1½ oz (45 g) sliced fresh mushrooms

1 oz (30 g) prosciutto or ham, chopped

2 plum (Roma) tomatoes, thinly sliced

4 teaspoons Pesto (page 65)

2 tablespoons grated Parmesan cheese

❖ For the crust, in a large saucepan of boiling salted water cook the pasta until al dente (8–12 minutes for dried pasta, 1–2 minutes for fresh pasta). Drain and return to the pan.

❖ Meanwhile, preheat an oven to 350°F (180°C/Gas Mark 4). In a medium mixing bowl combine the egg, Parmesan, and butter. Add to the hot pasta and toss to coat. Press the pasta mixture evenly over the base and side of a well-greased 9-inch (23-cm) pie plate.

❖ For the cheese filling, combine the egg, ricotta, and pepper in a small mixing bowl. Spread over the crust.

❖ For the topping, heat the olive oil in a medium frying pan and cook the mushrooms, stirring, until tender. Set aside. Sprinkle the prosciutto or ham over the cheese filling. Arrange the tomato slices in a circle, 1 inch (2.5 cm) from the edge of the pie plate. Dot the tomato slices with the pesto. Arrange the mushrooms inside the circle of tomatoes.

❖ Cover and bake for 20 minutes. Uncover and sprinkle with the Parmesan cheese. Bake, uncovered, for about 5 minutes more, or until the cheese melts. Set aside for 5–10 minutes before cutting into wedges to serve.

balsamic

broccoli, sausage, and pasta shells

serves 4

Italian balsamic vinegar is
aged for years in wooden
barrels to mellow and
sweeten. Look for this
unique condiment in
gourmet food shops and
well-stocked supermarkets.

6 oz (185 g) conchiglie, cavatelli,
or other shell-shaped pasta

8 oz (250 g) broccoli florets

12 oz (375 g) spicy Italian sausages

1 tablespoon olive oil

2 cloves garlic, peeled

1 tablespoon all-purpose (plain) flour

1/8–1/4 teaspoon crushed chile flakes

1 cup (8 fl oz/250 ml) chicken stock

2 tablespoons balsamic vinegar

❖ In a large saucepan of boiling salted water cook the pasta until al dente. Add the broccoli for the last 5 minutes of cooking. Drain and return the pasta and broccoli to the saucepan.

❖ Meanwhile, bring ½ cup (4 fl oz/125 ml) water to a boil in a large frying pan. Add the sausages and cook, covered, for 15 minutes. Drain off the liquid. Add the olive oil and garlic to the sausages and cook, uncovered, for 4–5 minutes, turning the sausages to brown them all over. Remove from the heat. Discard the garlic and drain off the pan drippings, reserving 1 tablespoon. Cool the sausages, then cut into ¼-inch (6-mm) thick pieces.

❖ Stir the flour and chile flakes into the reserved drippings in the pan. Add the stock and cook over medium heat, stirring, until the mixture boils and thickens. Boil, stirring, for 2 minutes more. Stir in the vinegar. Pour over the pasta and broccoli and toss to combine. Add the sausages and toss well. Heat over low heat until warmed through. Serve immediately.

lasagna verdi

serves 6–8

In Italian, verdi means "green," and green spinach pasta is what gives this recipe its name. You can use plain pasta if you prefer.

9 spinach-flavored lasagna noodles or 3 portions Spinach Pasta (pages 304–305)

1 quantity Bolognese Sauce (page 200)

2 tablespoons butter

2 tablespoons all-purpose (plain) flour

salt and ground black pepper

2/3 cup (5 fl oz/160 ml) milk

1/2 cup (4 oz/125 g) ricotta cheese

2 cups (8 oz/250 g) shredded mozzarella cheese

1/4 cup (1 oz/30 g) grated Parmesan cheese

❖ If using homemade pasta, roll out each portion of dough to a 12- x 9-inch (30- x 23-cm) rectangle. Cut each rectangle into three 12- x 2½-inch (30- x 6-cm) pieces.

❖ Prepare the bolognese sauce as directed (omit the extra parsley, Parmesan, and spaghetti). Set aside. In a small saucepan melt the butter. Stir in the flour, salt, and pepper. Add the milk and cook over medium heat, stirring, until the mixture boils and thickens. Stir in the ricotta.

❖ Preheat an oven to 375°F (190°C/Gas Mark 4). In a large saucepan of boiling salted water cook the pasta until al dente (10–12 minutes for dried pasta, 2–3 minutes for fresh). Drain and rinse with cold water; drain again.

❖ Spread ½ cup (4 fl oz/125 ml) of the Bolognese sauce over the base of a greased 8-cup (2-qt/2-l) rectangular baking dish. Arrange 3 of the noodles or 3 strips of fresh pasta on top of the sauce. Spread with half of the remaining Bolognese sauce. Sprinkle with half of the mozzarella and half of the Parmesan. Add another layer of pasta and spread the ricotta mixture over the top. Finish with another layer of pasta, then the remaining Bolognese sauce, mozzarella, and Parmesan. Bake, uncovered, for 30 minutes, or until heated through. Set aside for 10 minutes before serving.

pastitsio

serves 4

The white sauce firms up into a creamy, delicious layer, and the cinnamon adds an exotic flavour to this traditional Greek dish.

1 quantity Meat Sauce (page 146)

PASTA

8 oz (250 g) elbow macaroni

1 egg, beaten lightly

¼ cup (1 oz/30 g) grated Parmesan cheese

WHITE SAUCE

3 tablespoons butter

3 tablespoons all-purpose (plain) flour

¼ teaspoon pepper

1¼ cups (12 fl oz/375 ml) milk

1 egg, beaten lightly

¼ cup (1 oz/30 g) grated Parmesan cheese

ground cinnamon (optional)

❖ Prepare the meat sauce as directed. Set aside.

❖ Preheat an oven to 350°F (180°C/Gas Mark 4). For the pasta, bring a large saucepan of salted water to a boil. Add the pasta and cook until al dente. Drain and rinse with cold water; drain again. Place in a large mixing bowl and add the beaten egg and cheese. Mix to combine, and set aside.

❖ For the white sauce, melt the butter in a medium saucepan. Stir in the flour and pepper. Add the milk and cook, stirring, until the mixture boils and thickens. Stir about half of the mixture into the beaten egg. Return the egg mixture to the saucepan and stir in the cheese.

❖ Spread half of the pasta mixture in a greased 8-cup (2-qt/2-l) square baking dish. Top with the meat sauce, then the remaining pasta mixture. Spoon the white sauce over the top. Sprinkle lightly with the cinnamon, if desired.

❖ Bake for 30–35 minutes, or until the top has set. Set aside for 5 minutes before serving.

agnolotti florentine

Agnolotti ("fat little lambs") and ravioli are essentially the same dish, except the former are shaped into half-moons, while ravioli are square. The tomato- or spinach-flavored pasta complements the spinach filling and cheesy mornay sauce perfectly.

SPINACH AGNOLOTTI

1 quantity Tomato or Spinach Pasta (pages 304–305)

3 oz (90 g) packaged cream cheese with chives

5 oz (155 g) fresh spinach or frozen spinach, thawed, chopped, cooked, and well drained

1 egg yolk

1 oz (30 g) finely chopped prosciutto

2 tablespoons grated Parmesan cheese

pinch of ground nutmeg

MORNAY SAUCE

2 tablespoons butter

2 tablespoons all-purpose (plain) flour

1¼ cups (10 fl oz/315 ml) milk

1 cup (4 oz/125 g) shredded fontina or Jarlsberg cheese

❖ For the spinach agnolotti, prepare the fresh pasta as directed, except roll each portion of dough into an 8- x 12-inch (20- x 30-cm) rectangle. Cover and set aside. Bring the cream cheese to room temperature. Place the spinach and egg yolk in a food processor or blender and process or blend until nearly smooth. Transfer to a medium mixing bowl and stir in the cream cheese, prosciutto, Parmesan, and nutmeg. Cover and refrigerate until needed.

❖ Cut the pasta dough into circles using a 2-inch (5-cm) fluted cutter. Place about ½ teaspoon of filling on each pasta circle and brush the edges with water. Fold each circle in half to create half-moon shapes. Preheat an oven to 300°F (150°C/Gas Mark 2).

❖ For the mornay sauce, melt the butter in a small saucepan. Stir in the flour. Add the milk and cook over medium heat, stirring, until the mixture boils and thickens. Boil, stirring, for 1 minute more. Stir in the fontina or Jarlsberg cheese until melted. Keep warm.

❖ Meanwhile, in a large saucepan of boiling salted water cook the pasta until al dente, stirring occasionally. Do not crowd the agnolotti. Use a slotted spoon to transfer the pasta to a greased casserole. Cover and keep warm in preheated oven while cooking the remaining pasta. Serve the hot cooked pasta immediately, topped with the mornay sauce.

meat-stuffed
ravioli

serves 4

Using egg roll wrappers is a
good way to cut down on
the preparation time for this
recipe. Simply substitute
48 wrappers for the pasta
and cook for 6–8 minutes.

2 portions (8 oz/250 g) Homemade Pasta
(pages 304–305)

1 quantity Herb and Tomato Sauce (page 101)
or 28 fl oz (875 ml) canned or bottled
Italian-style tomato sauce

1 egg, beaten lightly

¾ cup (1½ oz/45 g) fresh bread crumbs

2 tablespoons dry red wine

1 clove garlic, finely chopped

1 teaspoon fennel seeds, crushed

¼ teaspoon Italian seasoning, crushed

salt and ground black pepper

12 oz (375 g) ground (minced) lean beef or veal

¼ cup (1 oz/30 g) grated Parmesan cheese

❖ Prepare the homemade pasta as directed, except roll each portion of dough into an 8- x 12- inch (20- x 30- cm) rectangle. Cover and set aside.

❖ If using the herb and tomato sauce, prepare as directed. Set aside.

❖ In a mixing bowl combine the egg, bread crumbs, wine, garlic, fennel seeds, Italian seasoning, salt, and pepper. Add the beef or veal and mix well. Shape the mixture into a flat 6- x 4-inch (15- x 10-cm) rectangle. Cut into 24 squares of 1 inch (2.5 cm). Preheat an oven to 300°F (150°C/Gas Mark 2).

❖ Cut each pasta rectangle into four 2- x 12-inch (5- x 30-cm) strips. Brush the side of 1 pasta strip with water. Place a square of meat mixture every 2 inches (5 cm), beginning 1 inch (2.5 cm) from the end of the strip. Top with a second pasta strip and press down around the meat squares. Use a 2-inch (5-cm) ravioli cutter, square cookie cutter, or sharp knife to cut out ravioli. Press the edges down firmly to seal. Repeat with the remaining pasta and meat mixture.

❖ In a large saucepan of boiling salted water cook half of the ravioli, uncovered, stirring occasionally, for 6–8 minutes, or until the meat inside is no longer pink and the pasta is al dente. Use a slotted spoon to transfer to a greased casserole. Cover and keep warm in the preheated oven while cooking the remaining ravioli. Serve the hot cooked ravioli topped with the tomato sauce and sprinkled with the cheese.

cheese tortellini
with sausage and bell peppers

serves 4

12 oz (375 g) Italian-style sausages

2 teaspoons olive oil

1 cup (4 oz/125 g) chopped onion

2 cloves garlic, finely chopped

28 oz (880 g) canned Italian-style tomatoes, cut up, with juice

1/4 cup (2 oz/60 g) tomato paste

1/4 cup (2 fl oz/60 ml) dry red wine

2 tablespoons chopped fresh parsley

1 teaspoon dried oregano, crushed

1/4 teaspoon crushed chile flakes

1 medium green bell pepper (capsicum), cut into 1/2-inch (13-mm) pieces

12 oz (375 g) dried or 1 lb (500 g) fresh cheese-filled tortellini, ravioli, or agnolotti

❖ Heat 1 cup (8 fl oz/250 ml) water in a large frying pan. Add the sausages and bring to a boil. Reduce heat, cover, and simmer for 15 minutes, or until the juices run clear when a skewer is inserted in the sausages. Drain off water. Cook the sausages, uncovered, turning often, for 2–4 minutes more, or until browned all over. Remove from pan and set aside to cool. Cut the sausages diagonally into ½-inch (13-mm) pieces. Wipe the pan clean with paper towels.

❖ In the same pan, heat the oil and cook the onion and garlic, stirring often, until just tender. Stir in the tomatoes, tomato paste, wine, parsley, oregano, and chile flakes. Stir in the sausage and bell pepper and bring to a boil. Reduce the heat, cover and simmer for 20 minutes, or until thickened to the desired consistency.

❖ Meanwhile, in a large saucepan of boiling salted water cook the pasta until al dente (15 minutes for dried pasta or 8–10 minutes for fresh). Drain and return to the saucepan. Add the sausage mixture and toss to combine. Serve immediately.

pasta
with
fish
and
seafood

trenette
with mussels and saffron

serves 4

*1 cup (8 fl oz/250 ml)
extra virgin olive oil*

1 clove garlic, finely chopped

*1 sprig fresh flat-leaf (Italian)
parsley, finely chopped*

*2 fresh mint leaves,
finely chopped*

*1 cup (3½ oz/105 g) cooked,
shelled mussels*

*13 oz (410 g) trenette
(thin ribbon pasta)*

4 pinches of saffron threads

❖ In a large frying pan heat the olive oil. Add the garlic, parsley, and mint and cook, stirring often, until the garlic is golden.

❖ Add the mussels and cook over medium heat, stirring often, for 2–3 minutes, or until heated through and well combined. Set aside.

❖ Meanwhile, in a large saucepan of boiling salted water cook the pasta until al dente; drain well. Add to the frying pan and stir carefully to coat the pasta with the mussel mixture.

❖ Serve topped with a pinch of saffron threads.

capri-style
linguine

serves 4–6

All around the Italian
coast, pasta dishes
with seafood are popular.
This one is typical of Capri,
and is perhaps the richest
of them all.

1 cup (8 fl oz/250 ml) extra virgin olive oil

13 oz (410 g) mussels, scrubbed and debearded

9 oz (280 g) clams, scrubbed

*6 oz (185 g) small uncooked shrimp
(green prawns); if heads are removed,
use an extra 3 oz (90 g) chopped shrimp*

*6 oz (185 g) small squid, cleaned and
cut into small strips*

2 cloves garlic, chopped

1 cup (8 fl oz/250 ml) dry white wine

*13 oz (410 g) ripe tomatoes,
peeled, seeded, and chopped*

salt and ground black pepper

8 oz (250 g) dried or 1 lb (500 g) fresh linguine

*2 tablespoons finely chopped fresh
flat-leaf (Italian) parsley*

❖ Heat 3 tablespoons of the olive oil in a large frying pan over high heat. Add the mussels and clams, cover, and cook for 4–5 minutes, or until most of the mussels and clams have opened. Discard any that are still closed. Remove the meat from the shells and set aside, reserving the liquid in the pan. Peel the shrimp and set aside. Crush the shrimp heads. Add the heads and shells to the frying pan, reduce the heat to low, and cook gently until the liquid is quite thick. Pour the mixture through a fine-mesh sieve into a bowl. Reserve the liquid; discard the solids.

❖ In a large saucepan combine the remaining oil, squid, and garlic. Add a little wine and cook, stirring, until it evaporates. Continue adding the wine in this way until all the wine has been added and evaporated. Add the tomatoes and season to taste with salt and pepper. Stir in half of the reserved cooking juices from the shellfish and cook over medium heat for 20 minutes. If the mixture dries out, add more of the reserved cooking juices. Stir in the shrimp and cook for 10 minutes more. Add the mussel and clam meat, stir well, and cook for 3–4 minutes, or until well combined and heated through.

❖ Meanwhile, in a large saucepan of boiling salted water cook the pasta until al dente; drain. Add the pasta to the seafood mixture and mix well. Serve sprinkled with pepper and parsley.

lobster
with bow-tie pasta

serves 4

½ cup (4 fl oz/125 ml)
extra virgin olive oil

2 cloves garlic, crushed

2 lobsters, about
1 lb (500 g) each

2 lb (1 kg) tomatoes,
peeled and quartered

salt

8 oz (250 g) dried farfalle
(bow-tie pasta)

crushed dried chile, to taste

2 tablespoons chopped fresh
flat-leaf (Italian) parsley

❖ Heat the olive oil in a large saucepan. Add the garlic and cook until lightly browned. Cut the lobsters up, crushing the nippers, and add to the pan. Cook, stirring often, for 15 minutes. Stir in the tomatoes and cook for 30 minutes. Season to taste with salt.

❖ Meanwhile, in a large saucepan of boiling salted water cook the pasta until al dente; drain. Divide the pasta among serving plates. Top each with a few pieces of lobster and some of the sauce. Serve immediately, sprinkled with a little chile and some parsley.

spaghetti with orange-anchovy sauce

serves 6

6½ oz (200 g) anchovies packed in salt

2 tablespoons olive oil

1 clove garlic, finely chopped

2 oranges, peeled, white pith removed, flesh diced

½ cup (2 oz/60 g) dried bread crumbs

½ cup (4 fl oz/125 ml) orange-flavored liqueur

salt

12 oz (375 g) spaghetti

1 bunch fresh mint leaves

❖ Wash the anchovies well to remove all the salt. Open them up and remove the backbones. Cut the anchovies into small pieces.

❖ Heat the olive oil in a frying pan. Add the garlic and cook briefly over low heat. Add the anchovies and use a fork to stir until the mixture has a creamy consistency.

❖ Stir in the oranges, bread crumbs, and orange liqueur. Season to taste with salt.

❖ Meanwhile, in a large saucepan of boiling salted water cook the pasta until al dente; drain. Divide the pasta among serving bowls, spoon the sauce over, and serve sprinkled with mint leaves.

sea bass ravioli
with clam sauce

serves 4

Only recently has fish been used in Italian stuffed pastas, beginning on the Tyrrhenian coast between Genoa and Leghorn, and from there taking off all over Italy. These days, you can find magnificent fish ravioli even in cities that are nowhere near the sea.

PASTA

1⅔ cups (7 oz/220 g) all-purpose (plain) flour

6 egg yolks, beaten together

1 tablespoon olive oil

1 tablespoon milk

pinch of salt

1 egg yolk, extra, beaten, for brushing

FILLING

¹/₂ cup (4 fl oz/125 ml) olive oil

10 oz (315 g) skinless sea bass fillets

2 oz (60 g) escarole (endive)

3 tablespoons dry white wine

3 tablespoons fish stock

*1 teaspoon chopped fresh
flat-leaf (Italian) parsley*

1 tablespoon extra virgin olive oil

salt and ground black pepper

SAUCE

¹/₂ cup (4 fl oz/125 ml) olive oil

1 clove garlic

1¹/₂ lb (750 g) baby clams, scrubbed

3 tablespoons dry white wine

*1 large tomato, peeled, seeded,
and chopped*

salt and ground black pepper

*1 teaspoon chopped fresh
flat-leaf (Italian) parsley*

❖ For the pasta, heap the flour onto a work surface and make a well in the center. Add the egg yolks, olive oil, milk, and salt to the flour. Mix to make a smooth dough. Roll the dough into a ball and set aside, covered with a damp kitchen towel.

❖ For the filling, heat the olive oil in a frying pan. Add the fish fillets, escarole, wine, and fish stock and stir to combine. Cover and cook over medium heat for 7 minutes. Remove from the heat and drain off the excess liquid. Finely chop the fish and escarole. Transfer to a small bowl and stir in the parsley and extra virgin olive oil. Season to taste with salt and pepper.

❖ Roll out the pasta dough into 2 thin, 12-inch (30-cm) squares, and brush with the extra beaten egg yolk. Place the filling on 1 pasta sheet in ¹/₂-teaspoon portions, 2 inches (5 cm) apart. Place the second

sea bass ravioli with clam sauce

pasta sheet on top and press down gently around each mound of filling. Use a ravioli wheel or fluted pastry wheel to cut into 2-inch (5-cm) square ravioli.

✥ For the sauce, heat the olive oil in a large frying pan. Add the garlic and cook, stirring often, until it is lightly browned. Add the clams, cover, and cook over high heat for 5 minutes. Set aside to cool, discarding any clams that do not open. Remove the meat from the shells. Strain and reserve the cooking liquid.

✥ In a large, shallow frying pan combine the clam meat and wine and cook until the wine evaporates. Stir in the tomato and the reserved cooking liquid. Season to taste with salt and pepper. Stir in the parsley and cook for 5 minutes.

✥ Meanwhile, in a large saucepan of boiling salted water cook the ravioli until they rise to the surface; drain well. Divide the ravioli among serving bowls, spoon over the hot sauce, and serve.

recipe hint

Escarole is a type of endive with broad leaves that are not quite as curly or bitter as chicory. The leaves have slightly bent edges, and the inner leaves are paler and not as bitter as the outer leaves. Although it is usually eaten raw, escarole may be cooked, as in this recipe.

fettuccine
with salmon and mushrooms

serves 4

1 tablespoon butter

3 green (spring) onions, finely chopped

8 oz (250 g) button mushrooms, wiped clean and sliced

1 cup (8 fl oz/250 ml) heavy (double) cream

1 tablespoon tomato paste

6½ oz (200 g) canned red salmon, drained, skin and bones removed, flesh flaked

1 lb (500 g) fettuccine

❖ Melt the butter in a large frying pan. Add the onions and gently cook, stirring often, until they are just tender. Add the mushrooms and cook, stirring often, for 2–3 minutes. Add the cream and tomato paste and stir over low heat until the tomato paste is completely mixed into the sauce. Stir in the salmon and simmer for 1–2 minutes.

❖ Meanwhile, in a large saucepan of boiling salted water cook the pasta until al dente. Drain well and add to the sauce. Mix to combine and serve immediately.

❖ Note: The sauce can be made 1–2 hours ahead and reheated gently when required.

orzo and tuna stuffed
bell peppers

serves 4

1/4 cup (2 fl oz/60 ml) olive oil

1 onion, finely chopped

2 cloves garlic, crushed

1 can (13 1/2 oz/425 g) plum
(Roma) tomatoes

1 tablespoon tomato paste

1 tablespoon chopped fresh basil

1 tablespoon chopped fresh oregano

1 tablespoon chopped fresh
flat-leaf (Italian) parsley

4 oz (125 g) orzo (risoni)

1 can (6 oz/185 g) tuna, preferably
Italian-style, drained and flaked

2 teaspoons tiny capers, well rinsed

8 black olives, pitted and chopped

2 large red bell peppers (capsicums)

6 1/2 oz (200 g) mozzarella cheese, sliced

1 can (2 oz/60 g) flat anchovy fillets

1 cup (4 oz/125 g) grated Parmesan cheese

ground black pepper

olive oil, extra, for sprinkling

✦ Heat half of the olive oil in a large saucepan. Add the onion and garlic and cook gently, stirring often, until the onion is soft. Stir in the undrained tomatoes, tomato paste, and herbs. Simmer, uncovered, for 25 minutes, or until the sauce thickens. Remove from the heat.

✦ Meanwhile, in a saucepan of boiling salted water cook the orzo until al dente. Drain well and cover to keep warm.

✦ Add the tuna, capers, olives, and orzo to the tomato mixture and stir to combine. Preheat an oven to 350°F (180°C/Gas Mark 4).

✦ Cut the bell peppers in half lengthwise, and remove the stems, seeds, and membranes. Arrange the bell peppers snugly in a baking dish, cut-side up, and spoon the pasta mixture into them. Smooth the surface, then drizzle the remaining oil over the top. Bake the stuffed bell peppers for 40 minutes.

✦ Remove the bell peppers from the oven and top with the mozzarella and then the anchovies in a criss-cross pattern. Sprinkle with the Parmesan, pepper, and a little extra oil. Return the bell peppers to the oven and bake for 10 minutes, or until the cheese is golden. Serve immediately.

macaroni cheese
with tuna and peas

serves 4–6

This dish can be made 1–2 days in advance and refrigerated in an airtight container. (If you are making the dish in advance, do not bake before storing.) Cook in an oven preheated to 350°F (180°C/Gas Mark 4).

1 tablespoon olive or vegetable oil

2 cups (7 oz/220 g) macaroni

vegetable oil or melted butter, for sprinkling

2 tablespoons butter

2 tablespoons all-purpose (plain) flour

1½ cups (12 fl oz/375 ml) milk

¾ cup (3 oz/90 g) grated Gruyère cheese

½ teaspoon sharp mustard

2 teaspoons chopped fresh parsley

1 can (6½ oz/200 g) tuna, drained and flaked

1 cup (5 oz/155 g) green peas, cooked until tender

¼ cup (1 oz/30 g) fine dried bread crumbs

✤ Preheat an oven to 350°F (180°C/Gas Mark 4).

✤ Bring a large saucepan of salted water to a simmer. Add the oil and pasta and simmer (making sure the water does not boil) until the pasta is tender but still holding its form. Drain and return to the pan. Sprinkle the pasta with a little vegetable oil or melted butter to prevent it from sticking together. Cover; keep warm.

✤ Melt the 2 tablespoons of butter in a medium saucepan. Stir in the flour and cook briefly, then whisk in the milk and cook, whisking, until the mixture boils and thickens. Stir in the cheese, mustard, and parsley.

✤ Add the tuna and peas to the pasta and stir to combine. Transfer to a buttered ovenproof dish and pour the sauce over. Sprinkle with the bread crumbs and dot with a little extra chopped butter, if desired. Bake for about 15 minutes, or until the surface is crisp and golden. Serve immediately.

recipe hint

If you would like to freeze this dish, place the unbaked macaroni cheese in an airtight container and wrap the container in several layers of plastic wrap. Transfer from the freezer to the refrigerator at least 5 hours (preferably overnight) before cooking.

pasta and prawn

diavolo

serves 4

"Diavolo" is synonymous with "spicy." You can easily adjust the spiciness of this dish by increasing or decreasing the amount of chile you use, or by adding some crushed chile flakes for a real kick.

8 oz (250 g) dried spaghetti, linguine, or fettuccine, or 1 lb (500 g) fresh linguine or fettuccine

4 oz (125 g) broccoli florets

1 cup (8 fl oz/250 ml) chicken stock

2 tablespoons cornstarch (cornflour)

2 tablespoons Dijon mustard

2 tablespoons fresh lemon juice

1 tablespoon capers, drained and rinsed

2 tablespoons olive oil

1 lb (500 g) uncooked shrimp (green prawns), peeled and deveined, or 12 oz (375 g) frozen peeled uncooked shrimp, thawed

½ teaspoon hot chile oil or ⅛ teaspoon chile powder

lemon wedges for garnish (optional)

❖ If you are using dried pasta, in a large saucepan of boiling salted water cook the pasta until al dente. During the last 5 minutes of cooking time, add the broccoli. Drain well. If you are using fresh pasta, cook the broccoli separately in a small amount of boiling water for 5 minutes, or until just tender. Drain and add to the drained, cooked pasta. Fresh pasta takes only 1½–2 minutes to cook, whereas dried pasta takes 8–12 minutes.

❖ Meanwhile, in a small mixing bowl combine the stock, cornstarch, mustard, lemon juice, and capers; set aside. Heat the olive oil in a large frying pan over medium-high heat and cook the prawns and chile oil or powder, stirring, for 1 minute. Stir the stock mixture and carefully add to the pan. Cook, stirring, until the mixture boils and thickens. Boil, stirring, for 2 minutes more, or until the prawns are opaque. Add to the pasta and broccoli and toss to combine. Serve immediately, garnished with lemon wedges, if desired.

8 oz (250 g) dried spaghetti
or 1 lb (500 g) fresh linguine
or fettuccine

6½ oz (200 g) cream cheese,
at room temperature

1 tablespoon chopped
fresh dill

6½ oz (200 g) smoked
salmon, diced

sprigs of fresh dill

lemon slices or wedges

❖ In a large saucepan of boiling salted water cook the pasta until al dente; drain.

❖ Meanwhile, place the cream cheese and dill in a small bowl. Using an electric mixer on medium speed, beat until combined.

❖ Stir the cream cheese mixture into the hot pasta. Serve immediately, topped with the salmon and dill sprigs, and accompanied by the lemon.

spaghetti
with smoked salmon
and cream cheese

pasta
with tapenade

serves 4

8 oz (250 g) cavatelli, conchiglie (pasta shells), or other shaped pasta

½ fennel bulb or 2 oz (60 g) celery, cut into ¼-inch (6-mm) thick slices

½ red bell pepper (capsicum), cut into thin strips

½ yellow bell pepper (capsicum), cut into thin strips

1 cup (4 oz/125 g) pitted black Greek or Niçoise olives

3½ oz (105 g) tuna, canned in water, drained

1 tablespoon capers, drained and rinsed

½ teaspoon dried oregano or thyme, crushed

1 teaspoon anchovy paste (optional)

1 clove garlic

1 tablespoon olive oil

1–2 teaspoons fresh lemon juice

2 tablespoons chopped fresh parsley

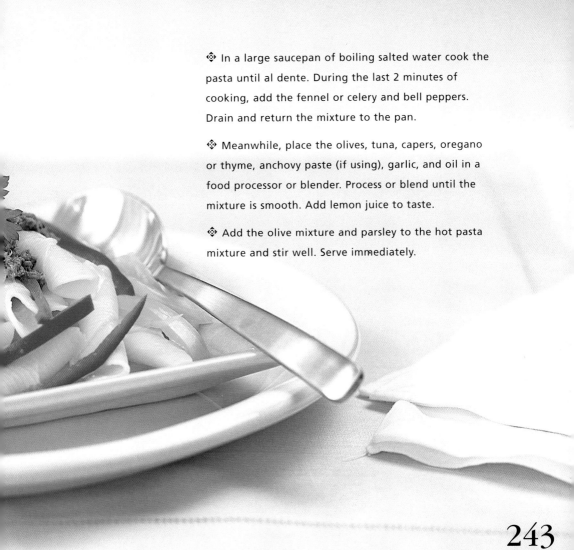

❖ In a large saucepan of boiling salted water cook the pasta until al dente. During the last 2 minutes of cooking, add the fennel or celery and bell peppers. Drain and return the mixture to the pan.

❖ Meanwhile, place the olives, tuna, capers, oregano or thyme, anchovy paste (if using), garlic, and oil in a food processor or blender. Process or blend until the mixture is smooth. Add lemon juice to taste.

❖ Add the olive mixture and parsley to the hot pasta mixture and stir well. Serve immediately.

243

scallops and penne in red sauce

serves 4

8 oz (250 g) penne, rigatoni,
or other shaped pasta

12 oz (375 g) fresh or thawed
frozen scallops

2 tablespoons olive oil

2 cloves garlic, finely chopped

½ cup (4 fl oz/125 ml) Vermouth
or red wine

2 teaspoons cornstarch (cornflour)

2 lb (1 kg) ripe plum (Roma) tomatoes,
peeled, seeded, and finely chopped

4 oz (125 g) bottled or canned diced pimiento, drained

2 tablespoons chopped fresh parsley

2 tablespoons chopped fresh basil

½ teaspoon salt

¼ teaspoon crushed chile flakes

¼ cup (1 oz/30 g) grated Parmesan cheese (optional)

❖ In a large saucepan of boiling salted water cook the pasta until al dente. Drain well.

❖ Meanwhile, halve the scallops, if large. Heat the oil in a large frying pan over medium heat, add the garlic, and cook, stirring, for 1 minute. Add the scallops and cook, stirring, for 2 minutes, or until the scallops are opaque. Remove the scallops from the pan; keep warm.

❖ Add the Vermouth or red wine and the cornstarch to the frying pan and stir well. Stir in the tomatoes, pimiento, parsley, basil, salt, and chile flakes. Cook, stirring, until the mixture boils and thickens. Boil, stirring, for 2 minutes. Add the hot pasta and scallops to the pan and mix well. Serve immediately, sprinkled with cheese, if desired.

245

tagliatelle
with zucchini flowers
and shrimp

serves 4

10 oz (315 g) dried tagliatelle

2 tablespoons olive oil

3 tablespoons butter

1 shallot, finely chopped

8 uncooked large shrimp
(green king prawns), peeled

12 zucchini (courgette)
flowers, cut into thin strips

salt and ground black pepper

½ cup (4 fl oz/125 ml) heavy
(double) cream

❖ In a large saucepan of boiling salted water cook the pasta until al dente; drain.

❖ Meanwhile, heat the oil and butter in a frying pan over medium heat. Add the shallot and cook, stirring, until it just browns. Add the shrimp and cook, stirring, for 4 minutes.

❖ Add the zucchini flowers to the frying pan and toss to combine. Add salt and pepper to taste. Stir in the cream, then remove from the heat. Spoon over the pasta and serve immediately.

247

salmon lasagne
with roasted bell pepper sauce

2 large red bell peppers (capsicums)

12 oz (375 g) skinless fresh or thawed frozen salmon fillets, or 12 oz (375 g) canned salmon, drained, skin and bones removed, flaked

9 lasagna noodles

½ cup (4 fl oz/125 ml) sour cream

1 tablespoon all-purpose (plain) flour

¼ teaspoon salt

⅛ teaspoon pepper

1 egg, beaten

1 cup (8 oz/250 g) ricotta cheese

1 cup (8 oz/250 g) cream cheese, softened

⅓ cup (2½ fl oz/80 ml) Pesto (page 65) or purchased pesto (optional)

❖ Preheat an oven to 425°F (210°C/Gas Mark 5).

❖ Halve the bell peppers lengthways and remove the stems, seeds, and membranes. Place the bell peppers, cut-side down, on a baking sheet lined with foil. Bake for 20–25 minutes, or until the skins blister and blacken. Transfer the bell peppers to a heatproof bowl and cover with plastic wrap. Set aside for about 10 minutes (this will make the skins easier to remove). Peel the bell peppers, discarding the skins. Reduce the oven temperature to 375°F (190°C/Gas Mark 4).

❖ Meanwhile, if using fresh or thawed frozen salmon fillets, in a large frying pan bring about 1½ cups (12 fl oz/375 ml) water to a boil. Measure the thickness of the fillets, then add them to the pan. Return to a boil. Reduce heat, cover, and simmer for 4–6 minutes for every ½-inch (13-mm) thickness. Drain well. Use a fork to gently break the salmon into bite-sized pieces. Set aside.

salmon lasagna
with roasted bell pepper sauce

✧ In a large saucepan of boiling salted water cook the pasta until al dente. Drain well. Rinse under cold running water, then drain again.

✧ In a food processor or blender, process or blend the roasted bell peppers until the mixture is almost smooth. Add the sour cream, flour, salt, and pepper. Process or blend until combined. Set aside.

✧ In a medium mixing bowl combine the egg, ricotta cheese, and cream cheese. Stir in the cooked or canned salmon.

✧ To assemble, lightly grease an 8-cup (2-qt/2-l) rectangular baking dish. Arrange 3 of the lasagna noodles in the base of the dish. Spread with a third of the cheese mixture. Repeat the layers twice. Carefully spread the roasted bell pepper mixture over the top. Bake, uncovered, for 30–35 minutes, or until the lasagne is heated through. Set aside for 10 minutes before serving. Serve with pesto, if desired.

pasta puttanesca

serves 6

1/2 cup (4 fl oz/125 ml) olive oil

3 cloves garlic, finely chopped

1 small fresh red chile, finely chopped (seeds included, if desired)

1 1/2 lb (750 g) tomatoes, peeled, seeded, and chopped

3/4 cup (4 oz/125 g) black olives, pitted and halved

1/4 cup (2 oz/60 g) capers, drained, rinsed, and finely chopped

5 oil-packed anchovy fillets, drained and chopped

1/3 cup (1/3 oz/10 g) fresh flat-leaf (Italian) parsley, finely chopped

1 tablespoon finely chopped fresh oregano

salt and ground black pepper

1 lb (500g) dried spaghetti

❖ Heat the oil in a large frying pan over medium heat. Add the garlic and cook, stirring, for 5 minutes or until it is golden. Add the chile and cook, stirring, for about 1 minute, or until it is fragrant. Add the tomatoes, olives, and capers and cook over medium-high heat, stirring occasionally, for 10 minutes. Stir in the anchovies, parsley, and oregano and cook for 2 minutes. Season to taste with salt and pepper.

❖ Meanwhile, in a large saucepan of boiling salted water cook the pasta until al dente. Drain, toss with the tomato mixture, and serve immediately.

seafood tagliatelle
with tomatoes and olives

serves 4

Tagliatelle, a classic pasta of
Bologna and the surrounding
Emilia-Romagna region in Italy,
forms a delicate bed for this
creamy sauce with shrimp and
scallops. Fettuccine, which is
slightly thicker and narrower than
tagliatelle, may be substituted.

8 oz (250 g) dried or 1 lb (500 g) fresh
tagliatelle or fettuccine

SAUCE

1 tablespoon sweet (unsalted) butter

2 tablespoons finely chopped shallots

2 cups (16 fl oz/500 ml) heavy
(double) cream

¼ cup (2 fl oz/60 ml) dry
Italian white wine

6 oz (185 g) uncooked medium shrimp
(medium green prawns), peeled, deveined,
and cut in half lengthwise

4 oz (125 g) scallops, sliced crosswise
into ¼-inch (6-mm) thick strips

½ cup (4 oz/125 g) drained oil-packed
sun-dried tomatoes, cut into thin strips

½ cup (3 oz/90 g) black olives,
pitted and cut in half

½ cup (2 oz/60 g) grated Parmesan cheese

salt and ground white pepper

grated nutmeg

❖ For the sauce, melt the butter in a large
frying pan over medium heat. Add the
shallots and cook, stirring often, until they
are almost translucent, about 3 minutes.
Stir in the cream and bring the mixture to
a boil. Reduce the heat to medium and
simmer, uncovered, until the sauce thickens
slightly, about 6 minutes. Stir in the wine
and simmer for 1 minute.

❖ Meanwhile, in a large saucepan of
boiling salted water cook the pasta until
al dente. Drain and return to the saucepan.

❖ While the pasta is cooking, add the
shrimp, scallops, and sun-dried tomatoes to
the sauce. Stir to combine and simmer for
1 minute. Stir in the olives and cheese.
Season to taste with salt, white pepper, and
nutmeg. Increase the heat to high and bring
the mixture to a boil.

seafood tagliatelle with tomatoes and olives

❖ Add the cooked pasta to the sauce. Toss well to combine and cook briefly until the pasta is hot and thoroughly coated in the sauce.

❖ Serve immediately, accompanied by a green salad or crusty Italian bread, if desired.

recipe variations

If you prefer, you can use firm white-fleshed fish fillets instead of the shrimp and scallops. Simply cut the fish into bite-sized pieces and add to the sauce; otherwise, the order of procedure and cooking times are the same.

anchovy spaghetti

serves 6

1¼ lb (625 g) fresh anchovies,
or 3 oz (90 g) anchovies
packed in salt, rinsed

1 lb (500 g) ripe plum
(Roma) tomatoes, peeled

salt

⅓ cup (2½ fl oz/80 ml)
extra virgin olive oil

1 clove garlic, crushed

½ cup (4 fl oz/125 ml)
dry white wine

1 cup (1 oz/30 g) finely
chopped fresh parsley

1¼ lb (625 g) spaghetti

❖ If using fresh anchovies, use a small, sharp knife to make a cut along the underside of each anchovy and remove the innards. Lift out the backbones and remove the heads. Wash under cold water and drain on paper towels. Cut the fresh or salt-packed anchovies into small pieces, reserving a few whole ones for the garnish. Roughly chop the tomatoes, then place in a fine-mesh sieve and sprinkle with a little salt. Set aside.

❖ Heat the olive oil in a large frying pan and cook the garlic until it begins to color. Stir in the anchovies and wine. Season with salt and stir in the tomatoes. Cook for 10 minutes. Stir in the parsley and keep warm.

❖ Meanwhile, in a large saucepan of boiling salted water cook pasta until al dente; drain. Stir in anchovy sauce. Serve garnished with the whole anchovies.

pasta and prawns
in asparagus sauce

serves 4

When setting aside some asparagus pieces before puréeing, choose only the tips, which are usually the most tender part of the stalk and are also the most attractive.

1½ lb (750 g) asparagus

8 oz (250 g) gemelli, rotini, or other shaped pasta

12 oz (375 g) fresh or thawed frozen uncooked shrimp (green prawns), peeled and deveined

1 cup (8 fl oz/250 ml) chicken stock

¼ cup (2 fl oz/60 ml) sour cream

2 tablespoons all-purpose (plain) flour

¼ teaspoon salt

⅛ teaspoon white pepper

1 tablespoon fresh lemon juice

❖ Snap off and discard the woody ends of the asparagus spears. Cut the asparagus into 2-inch (5-cm) pieces. Cook, covered, in a small amount of boiling water for 6–8 minutes, or until bright green and just tender. Drain, reserving ¼ cup (2 fl oz/60 ml) of the cooking liquid. Set aside 4 oz (125 g) of the asparagus pieces; keep warm. Place the remaining asparagus in a blender or food processor with the reserved cooking liquid and purée until almost smooth.

❖ Meanwhile, in a large saucepan of boiling salted water cook the pasta until al dente, 8–10 minutes. During the last 3 minutes of cooking, add the prawns to the saucepan. When the pasta is al dente and the prawns are opaque, drain well. Return the pasta and prawns to the saucepan and add the reserved asparagus pieces. Cover to keep warm.

❖ In a medium saucepan combine the stock, sour cream, flour, salt, and pepper. Add the asparagus purée and lemon juice and stir to combine. Cook over medium heat, stirring often, until the mixture boils and thickens. Boil, stirring, for 1 minute more. Pour the sauce over the hot pasta mixture and toss to coat. Serve immediately.

creamy clam
spaghetti

serves 4

This creamy version of the
ever-popular pasta with clam
sauce is cooked in minutes.
If small cans of minced
clams are pantry staples,
you can prepare an enticing
meal with very little notice.
Serve with a green salad
and some crusty bread to
soak up the sauce.

8 oz (250 g) dried spaghetti or linguine or
1 lb (500 g) fresh linguine or other ribbon pasta

SAUCE

14 oz (440 g) canned minced clams or
chopped cooked clams

1¾ cups (14 fl oz/440 ml) light (single) cream
or milk (less if using canned minced clams)

2 tablespoons butter

½ cup (2 oz/60 g) chopped onion

2 cloves garlic, finely chopped

¼ cup (1 oz/30 g) all-purpose (plain) flour

½ teaspoon dried basil or oregano, crushed

salt and ground black pepper

2 tablespoons chopped fresh parsley

¼ cup (2 fl oz/60 ml) dry white wine

¼ cup (1 oz/30 g) grated Parmesan cheese (optional)

In a large saucepan of boiling salted water cook the pasta until al dente (8–12 minutes for dried pasta or 1–2 minutes for fresh pasta). Drain well.

Meanwhile, for the sauce, if you are using canned minced clams, drain the clams, reserving the liquid. Add enough cream or milk to the liquid to make 1¾ cups (14 fl oz/440 ml). If you are using cooked clams, use 1¾ cups (14 fl oz/440 ml) cream or milk.

Melt the butter in a medium saucepan and cook the onion and garlic, stirring often, for 5 minutes, or until the onion is soft but not brown. Stir in the flour, basil or oregano, salt, and pepper. Stir in the cream mixture and cook, stirring often, until the mixture boils and thickens. Boil, stirring, for 1 minute more. Stir in the parsley, wine, and clams. Heat through.

Spoon the sauce over the hot pasta. Sprinkle with the cheese, if desired, and serve immediately.

recipe hint

Clams have two very hard shells that are hinged at one side. They are especially delicious when prepared with shallots, white wine, lemon, tomatoes, and/or thyme. Clams can be used to replace mussels, oysters, and scallops in most recipes.

pasta salads

filled pasta shell salad

serves 4

FILLING

2 small fresh chiles, finely chopped

1 clove garlic, crushed

2 tablespoons olive oil

1 tablespoon balsamic vinegar

juice of 4 limes

13 oz (410 g) butternut squash (pumpkin)

1 large red (Spanish) onion, diced

½ large red bell pepper (capsicum), diced

8 oz (250 g) giant pasta shells

2 tablespoons finely chopped cilantro
(fresh coriander) leaves

1 tablespoon finely chopped fresh chervil
or parsley

❖ For the filling, whisk together the chiles, garlic, olive oil, vinegar, and lime juice.

❖ Cut the squash into slices and steam until just tender; cool. Peel and cut into small dice.

❖ In a bowl, combine the squash, onion, bell pepper, and two-thirds of the lime mixture. Mix well, then set aside.

❖ In a large saucepan of boiling salted water cook the pasta until al dente. Drain and rinse under cold water; allow to cool.

❖ Spoon the filling into the pasta shells and drizzle with the remaining lime mixture. Serve sprinkled with the cilantro and chervil.

hero pasta salad

serves 4

SALAD

3 oz (90 g) rotini, cavatelli, or
other shaped pasta

4 oz (125 g) cubed provolone cheese

2 oz (60 g) ham, cut into thin,
bite-sized strips

2 oz (60 g) spicy salami, chopped

1 small red (Spanish) onion,
halved and then sliced

4 oz (125 g) pepperoncini (Tuscan pepper),
sliced, or sliced bell pepper (capsicum)

6 oz (185 g) shredded iceberg or
romaine (cos) lettuce

1 large tomato, coarsely chopped, or
4 oz (125 g) cherry tomatoes, halved

DRESSING

3 tablespoons olive or salad oil

3 tablespoons balsamic vinegar

1 tablespoon chopped fresh oregano or
1/2 teaspoon dried oregano, crushed

2 small cloves garlic, finely chopped

1/4 teaspoon dry mustard

1/8 teaspoon ground black pepper

❖ For the salad, in a large saucepan of boiling salted water cook the pasta until al dente; drain. Rinse with cold water and drain again thoroughly.

❖ In a large bowl toss together the cooked pasta, cheese, ham, salami, onion, and pepperoncini or bell pepper. Add the lettuce and tomato; gently toss to mix.

❖ For the dressing, combine the olive or salad oil, vinegar, oregano, garlic, mustard, and pepper in a screw-top jar. Cover and shake well. Pour over the salad just before serving and toss to combine.

recipe variations

This salad lends itself well to improvization. Try adding some sliced black olives, capers, chopped bell pepper (capsicum), or yellow or orange tomatoes. If you are making the salad ahead of time, add the lettuce, tomato and dressing just before serving to prevent the salad from becoming soggy.

grilled tuna and white bean salad

serves 4–6

12 oz (375 g) fresh or thawed frozen tuna steaks, ½ inch (12 mm) thick, or 12 oz (375 g) canned tuna, drained and broken into chunks

olive oil, for brushing

8 oz (250 g) penne or other shaped pasta

1¼ lb (625 g) canned cannellini or white kidney beans, drained and rinsed

2 medium tomatoes, coarsely chopped

½ medium yellow bell pepper (capsicum), cut into thin, bite-sized strips

½ cup (4 fl oz/125 ml) olive or salad oil

¼ cup (2 fl oz/60 ml) fresh lemon juice

2 green (spring) onions, finely chopped

2 tablespoons chopped fresh basil or 1 teaspoon dried basil, crushed

¼ teaspoon salt

⅛ teaspoon pepper

❖ If using fresh or thawed frozen tuna, measure the thickness of the steaks. Brush the tuna steaks with olive oil on both sides. Cook under a hot broiler (griller) for 4–6 minutes per ½-inch (13-mm) thickness, turning once, or until the tuna flakes easily when tested with a fork. Slice the tuna diagonally into thin strips.

❖ In a large saucepan of boiling salted water cook the pasta until al dente. Drain well.

❖ In a large bowl combine the cooked fresh or canned tuna, cooked pasta, beans, tomatoes, and bell pepper.

❖ In a screw-top jar combine the olive or salad oil, lemon juice, green onions, basil, salt, and pepper. Pour over the pasta mixture, toss gently, and serve.

recipe hint

If you have any leftover salad, store it in an airtight container in the refrigerator, but be sure to bring it back to room temperature before serving or the dressing will be thick and lumpy.

eggplant
salad shells

makes 18 shells

¼ cup (2 fl oz/60 ml) olive oil

1 medium eggplant (aubergine), peeled and
cut into ½-inch (13-mm) cubes

1½ oz (45 g) chopped onion

1½ oz (45 g) chopped celery

1 can (13½ oz/425 g) chopped tomatoes

3 tablespoons red wine vinegar

2 tablespoons tomato paste

1 teaspoon sugar

½ teaspoon salt

pinch of cayenne pepper

1 tablespoon chopped fresh parsley

1 tablespoon capers, drained and rinsed

½ cup (2½ oz/75 g) sliced pitted black
or Kalamata olives

2 tablespoons toasted pine nuts
or chopped almonds

18 conchiglioni (large pasta shells),
about 4 oz (125 g)

❖ Heat the olive oil in a large frying pan over medium heat. Add the eggplant, onion, and celery and cook, covered, stirring occasionally, for 5–8 minutes, or until just tender. Stir in the undrained tomatoes, vinegar, tomato paste, sugar, salt, and cayenne pepper. Cook, uncovered, over low heat, stirring occasionally, for 5 minutes, or until thickened to the desired consistency. Remove from the heat and stir in the parsley and capers. Cool, then cover and refrigerate for 2–24 hours.

❖ Remove the eggplant mixture from the refrigerator and set aside for 30 minutes. Stir in the olives and pine nuts or almonds.

❖ Meanwhile, in a large saucepan of boiling salted water cook the pasta until al dente; drain. Rinse with cold water, then drain again thoroughly. Pat dry with paper towels.

❖ Fill each pasta shell with the eggplant mixture. Serve immediately as an appetizer or with a selection of antipasto dishes.

pasta
salad niçoise

serves 4–6

DRESSING

2 tablespoons red wine vinegar

1 tablespoon fresh lemon juice

1 teaspoon Dijon mustard

1/2 teaspoon sugar

1 clove garlic, crushed

salt and ground black pepper

1/2 cup (4 fl oz/125 ml) olive oil

1/4 cup (2 fl oz/60 ml) olive oil, extra

1 clove garlic, crushed

*10 oz (315 g) fresh tuna,
skin removed, cut into slices
1/2 inch (13 mm) thick*

8 oz (250 g) shell pasta

*8 oz (250 g) green beans, trimmed, cut into
2-inch (5-cm) lengths, and blanched*

10 oz (315 g) cherry tomatoes

*6 1/2 oz (200 g) yellow teardrop (pear)
tomatoes (optional)*

3 1/2 oz (105 g) small black olives

*1 jar (6 oz/185 g) marinated artichoke
hearts, drained and halved*

*1 tablespoon each chopped fresh
parsley, basil, and chives*

1 can (2 oz/60 g) anchovy fillets, drained

4 hard-boiled eggs, peeled and quartered

✥ For the dressing, place the vinegar, lemon juice, mustard, sugar, garlic, salt, pepper, and olive oil in a screw-top jar and shake well.

✥ Heat the extra olive oil in a frying pan and cook the garlic, stirring, for 30 seconds. Add the tuna and cook gently for 1–2 minutes on each side, until it is seared but still rare in the middle. Transfer to paper towels to drain; allow to cool.

✥ In a large saucepan of boiling salted water cook the pasta until al dente; drain. Rinse and drain again.

✥ Place the tuna, cooked pasta, beans, tomatoes, olives, artichokes, herbs, and anchovies in a large bowl and toss gently to combine. Add the desired quantity of dressing. Stir carefully and thoroughly to coat all the ingredients with the dressing. Gently stir in the eggs.

recipe variations

If fresh tuna is unavailable, the same quantity of canned tuna may be used instead. Do not cook, simply drain well, flake into chunks, and add to the salad.

shell pasta
with basil vinaigrette

serves 4

VINAIGRETTE

1 cup (1 oz/30 g) loosely packed
fresh basil leaves

2 small cloves garlic, chopped

1 tablespoon red wine vinegar

salt and ground black pepper

1/4 cup (2 fl oz/60 ml) olive oil

8 oz (500 g) small pasta shells

6 1/2 oz (200 g) goat's milk cheese, crumbled

6 1/2 oz (200 g) cherry tomatoes, halved

3 1/2 oz (105 g) small black olives

4 wedges of focaccia

2 tablespoons olive oil

3 tablespoons toasted pine nuts

❖ For the vinaigrette, process the basil, garlic, vinegar, salt, and pepper in a food processor until the basil is finely chopped. Gradually add the 1/4 cup (2 fl oz/60 ml) olive oil and process until well combined.

❖ In a large saucepan of boiling salted water cook the pasta until al dente; drain. Rinse and drain again. Toss through enough vinaigrette to coat. Stir in cheese, tomatoes, and olives. Add more vinaigrette, if needed.

❖ Toast the focaccia, then brush with the 2 tablespoons of olive oil. Top the focaccia with the pasta mixture and serve sprinkled with the pine nuts.

individual tortellini salads

serves 4

1 lb (500 g) purchased tortellini filled
with ham and ricotta

SALAD

6¹/₂ oz (200 g) cherry tomatoes

3¹/₂ oz (105 g) small black olives

1 bunch arugula (rocket), washed and dried

1 cup (1 oz/30 g) shredded fresh basil

6¹/₂ oz (200 g) spicy salami, thinly shredded

2 small red (Spanish) onions, cut into rings

10 sun-dried tomatoes, cut into strips

¹/₂ cup (2 oz/60 g) Parmesan cheese shavings

DRESSING

¹/₂ cup (4 fl oz/125 ml) extra virgin olive oil

2 tablespoons balsamic vinegar

1 small clove garlic, crushed

salt and ground black pepper

❖ In a large saucepan of boiling salted water cook the tortellini until tender; drain.

❖ Meanwhile, for the dressing, combine all the dressing ingredients in a screw-top jar.

❖ Transfer the tortellini to a shallow baking dish. Pour over two-thirds of the dressing and gently toss the tortellini to coat. Allow the tortellini to cool to room temperature.

❖ Arrange the tortellini, tomatoes, olives, arugula, basil, salami, onion rings, and sun-dried tomatoes on individual serving plates. Top with the Parmesan shavings.

❖ Just before serving, drizzle each salad with a little more dressing.

shrimp salad
with red bell pepper mayonnaise

serves 4–6

The additions of macadamia
nuts and mango make this
shrimp pasta salad anything
but ordinary. Serve with
chilled white wine and
a crusty loaf of bread for a
simple yet elegant meal.

2 red bell peppers (capsicums), about 1 lb (500 g)
total weight

1 cup (8 fl oz/250 ml) good-quality,
whole-egg mayonnaise

8 oz (250 g) pasta shells

5 oz (155 g) snow peas (mangetouts)

2 medium avocados

juice of ½ lemon

4 green (spring) onions, diagonally sliced

1 cup (3½ oz/105 g) macadamia nuts,
roughly chopped and lightly toasted

2 mangoes, cut into bite-sized pieces

1 lb (500 g) cooked large shrimp (cooked king prawns),
peeled and deveined

snow pea (mangetout) sprouts, for garnish

❖ Cut the bell peppers in half lengthwise and remove the stems, seeds, and membranes. Place, cut-side down, under a hot broiler (griller) and cook until the skin is blackened and blistered. Transfer to a heatproof bowl and cover with plastic wrap (this helps loosen the skins). Set aside until cool. Peel, then roughly chop the flesh and place in a food processor. Process until smooth. Stir into the mayonnaise.

❖ In a large saucepan of boiling salted water cook the pasta until al dente. Drain and rinse under cold water. Drain again.

❖ Blanch the snow peas briefly in boiling water, then rinse under cold running water. Cut into thin diagonal strips. Cut the avocados in half, remove the stones, and peel away the skin. Cut the flesh into bite-sized pieces and toss in the lemon juice.

❖ In a large bowl combine the snow peas, avocados, green onions, half of the macadamia nuts, the mangoes, and shrimp. Toss through enough of the mayonnaise to coat the ingredients thoroughly. Serve garnished with the remaining macadamia nuts and the snow pea sprouts.

warm
tomato–feta salad

serves 4–6

Kalamata olives will give a stronger and more authentic Greek flavor than pitted black olives. Any leftover salad can be stored in an airtight container in the refrigerator, but make sure you bring it back to room temperature before serving.

3 ripe tomatoes or 6 ripe plum (Roma) tomatoes, seeded and chopped

3 tablespoons olive or salad oil

3 tablespoons fresh lemon juice

½ cup (½ oz/15 g) chopped fresh oregano or 1 teaspoon dried oregano, crushed

2 cloves garlic, finely chopped

⅛ teaspoon pepper

½ cup (2 oz/60 g) Kalamata olives, pitted and chopped, or pitted black olives, chopped

8 oz (250 g) crumbled feta cheese

8 oz (250 g) farfalle (bow-tie pasta) or pasta shells

❖ Drain the chopped tomatoes in a colander for about 15 minutes to remove the excess liquid.

❖ In a large mixing bowl whisk the olive or salad oil into the lemon juice. Stir in the oregano, garlic, and pepper. Add the drained tomatoes, olives, and cheese. Toss to combine. Set aside at room temperature for 30 minutes to let the flavors develop.

❖ Meanwhile, in a large saucepan of boiling salted water cook the pasta until al dente. Drain and return to the pan. Add the tomato mixture and toss to combine. Serve immediately.

recipe variations

This pasta salad is open to variations. Try adding capers, chopped stuffed green olives, and/or marinated artichoke hearts; replacing the oregano with basil or thyme; or using bocconcini instead of feta.

pasta salad
with walnut dressing

serves 4

8 oz (250 g) tricolored or plain radiatori or fusilli (spiral pasta)

1 cup (4 oz/125 g) chopped toasted walnuts

4 oz (125 g) coppa, ham, or prosciutto, cut into small cubes

4 oz (125 g) crumbled basil-and-tomato-flavored feta cheese or plain feta cheese

2½ oz (75 g) pitted black or green olives

¼ cup (2 fl oz/60 ml) olive or salad oil

¼ cup (2 fl oz/60 ml) fresh lime juice

½ cup (½ oz/15 g) chopped fresh parsley

1 clove garlic, finely chopped

¼ teaspoon salt

⅛ teaspoon pepper

red-tipped (oak) leaf lettuce, for serving

❖ In a large saucepan of boiling salted water cook the pasta until al dente. Drain well. Rinse under cold water, then drain again thoroughly.

❖ In a large bowl toss the cooked pasta with the walnuts, coppa, ham or prosciutto, cheese, and olives until well combined.

❖ Place the olive or salad oil, lime juice, parsley, garlic, salt, and pepper in a small screw-top jar and shake well to combine. Pour over the pasta mixture and gently toss to coat all the ingredients with the dressing. Serve the salad on lettuce leaves.

tortellini-mozzarella salad

serves 2–4

5 oz (155 g) dried or 10 oz (315 g) fresh meat-filled tortellini

6 oz (185 g) cubed plain or smoked mozzarella cheese

½ medium red or yellow bell pepper (capsicum), cubed

½ cup (½ oz/15 g) chopped fresh basil or 1 teaspoon dried basil, crushed

3 tablespoons olive or salad oil

2 tablespoons white wine vinegar

1 tablespoon balsamic vinegar

1 small head of radicchio, divided into leaf cups, or 4 large lettuce leaves

❖ In a large saucepan of boiling salted water cook the pasta until al dente (15 minutes for dried pasta and 8–10 minutes for fresh pasta). Drain well. Rinse under cold water, then drain again thoroughly.

❖ In a medium mixing bowl combine the cooked pasta, cheese, and bell pepper.

❖ Place the basil, olive or salad oil, white wine vinegar, and balsamic vinegar in a screw-top jar and shake well to combine. Pour over the pasta mixture and gently toss to coat all the ingredients with the dressing. Serve the salad in radicchio leaf cups or large lettuce leaves.

pasta *from the* microwave

microwave spaghetti bolognese

serves 4

4 slices bacon, finely chopped

1 onion, chopped

2 cloves garlic, crushed

11 oz (345 g) ground (minced) beef

1 medium carrot, peeled and grated

1 can (13 oz/410 g) tomatoes

2 teaspoons each of chopped
fresh marjoram and oregano

1 tablespoon chopped fresh parsley

2 tablespoons tomato paste

1 tablespoon Worcestershire sauce

ground black pepper

3 oz (90 g) fresh mushrooms, chopped

8 oz (250 g) spaghetti

grated Parmesan cheese

❖ Put bacon, onion, and garlic in a 12-cup (3-qt/3-l) microwave-safe casserole. Cook, covered, on high (100%) for 3 minutes. Stir in the beef, using a fork to break up lumps. Cook, covered, on high for 5 minutes, or until brown. Drain off fat. Stir in the carrot, tomatoes, herbs, tomato paste, Worcestershire sauce, and pepper. Cook, covered, on medium-high (70%) for 15 minutes, stirring every 5 minutes. Stir in the mushrooms. Cook on high for 3 minutes.

❖ Meanwhile, in a large saucepan of boiling salted water cook the pasta until al dente; drain. Serve topped with the sauce and sprinkled with the cheese.

cooking pasta in the microwave

Pasta will cook well in the microwave oven. However, it does not cook any more quickly, and because of the amount of water required for cooking pasta it is only possible to cook 250 g (8 oz) at a time. It is usually better to cook the accompanying sauce by microwave while the pasta cooks on the stovetop.

To cook pasta, use a casserole of at least 3 l (3 qt) capacity. For 250 g (8 oz) of dried pasta, add 6 cups (1.5 l) boiling water, salt to taste, and 1 tablespoon olive oil. Bring the water back to the boil on high (100%), stirring several times, and cook, uncovered, on high for 8–10 minutes. Drain, return to cooking container or a heated serving dish, add a little oil, and stir lightly if not serving immediately. (If using fresh pasta, cook for only 4–6 minutes.)

It is not possible to give accurate times for cooking pasta. Different brands of the same pasta have varying cooking times; cooking times will also vary according to the power of your microwave oven. Test the pasta after the minimum suggested time and continue cooking if necessary.

Always remember to allow enough time for boiling the water, as well as for cooking the pasta, otherwise the microwave part of the meal will be done far ahead of the pasta.

The recipes in this book have been tested using a 650-watt oven. If your oven uses a different wattage, adjust the cooking times accordingly. If in doubt, always be guided by your oven's instruction manual.

freezing pasta and sauce

Cooked pasta that has been frozen and defrosted does not have the same quality as freshly cooked pasta. If you need to freeze pasta, place it in a container just large enough for the quantity of pasta. (If put in too large a container, the pasta tends to dehydrate and may develop an unpleasant texture.)

Alternatively, pack the pasta in freezer bags in the quantities in which you plan to use it at a later stage. Extract as much air as possible, twist the bag closed, and secure with a metal tie.

defrosting and reheating pasta

If you have time, defrost the pasta by leaving it at room temperature for a few hours, or overnight in the refrigerator, then reheating gently but thoroughly in the microwave oven. A quicker method of

defrosting is as follows: Remove the metal tie but leave the bag closed, simply tucking under the end and placing on a plate. Heat on the defrost setting (30%) until the pasta is thawed and hot, moving the pasta several times by pushing the bag gently with a wooden spoon to assist even heating, without uncovering the pasta. The trapped steam does a dual job of hastening the thawing and keeping the pasta moist.

Tomato-based pasta sauces, too, can be successfully frozen with very little deterioration in quality. Freeze in portion-sized containers and defrost as described above. (Remember that sauce in a large, flat container will take less time to defrost than that in a small, deep container.) After defrosting, bring the sauce to a boil, then reduce the heat and simmer for at least 3 minutes. Freezing cream-based sauces is not recommended, as the cream tends to separate as it defrosts.

spaghetti with tuna

serves 4

8 oz (250 g) spaghetti

¼ cup (1 oz/30 g) all-purpose (plain) flour

1 cup (4 oz/125 g) grated Cheddar cheese

1 small onion, grated or finely chopped

1 clove garlic, crushed

1½ cups (12 fl oz/375 ml) dry white wine or a mixture of white wine and stock

1 can (13½ oz/425 g) tuna, drained and roughly flaked

½ teaspoon curry powder

6 stuffed green olives, roughly chopped

❖ In a large saucepan of boiling salted water cook the pasta until al dente. Drain and cover to keep warm.

❖ Meanwhile, combine the flour and cheese in a 4–8 cup (1–2 qt/1–2 l) microwave-safe dish or jug. Add the onion, garlic, and wine or wine mixture to the jug and stir into the cheese mixture. Heat on medium (50%) for 3 minutes. Stir well, then cook on medium for 5–6 minutes more, stirring occasionally, until the cheese has melted and the mixture is thick. Beat with a wooden spoon or whisk until the mixture is smooth. Stir in the tuna, curry powder, and olives. Heat on medium for 3–4 minutes, or until the ingredients are heated through.

❖ Serve the sauce spooned over the hot pasta.

spaghetti siciliana

serves 4

8 oz (250 g) spaghetti

2 tablespoons olive oil

4 tomatoes

1 red and 1 green
bell pepper (capsicum)

6 green (spring) onions,
finely chopped

¼ cup (1½ oz/45 g) black
olives, seeded and chopped

2 tablespoons green
olives, chopped

1 can (1½ oz/45 g) anchovy
fillets, chopped

ground black pepper

juice of ½ lemon

chopped fresh parsley

grated Parmesan cheese

❖ In a large saucepan of boiling salted water cook the pasta until al dente. Drain, drizzle with the oil, and toss to coat the pasta with the oil.

❖ Meanwhile, immerse the tomatoes in boiling water for 30 seconds. Drain; peel and chop. Halve the bell peppers lengthwise and remove the stems, seeds, and membranes; chop the flesh. Combine the tomatoes, bell peppers, onions, olives, anchovies, pepper, and lemon juice in a 12-cup (3-qt/3-l) microwave-safe dish. Cover and cook on high (100%) for 5 minutes, or until the mixture is boiling, stirring well after 2–3 minutes.

❖ Add the pasta to the tomato mixture. Cover and heat on high for 3–4 minutes, until heated through.

❖ Serve immediately, sprinkled with the chopped parsley and grated cheese.

tortellini
with cream sauce

serves 3–4

8 oz (250 g) tortellini

1 tablespoon butter

4 slices bacon, chopped

1 green bell pepper (capsicum), stemmed, seeded, and sliced

5 oz (155 g) fresh mushrooms, wiped clean and sliced

1 tablespoon all-purpose (plain) flour

2 teaspoons dry mustard

ground black pepper

1 cup (8 fl oz/250 ml) milk

½ cup (4 fl oz/125 ml) cream

½ cup (2 oz/60 g) grated cheddar or Parmesan cheese

❖ In a large saucepan of boiling salted water cook the pasta until al dente. Drain and cover to keep warm.

❖ Meanwhile, melt the butter in a shallow 4-cup (1-qt/1-liter) microwave-safe dish on high (100%) for 1 minute. Add the bacon and bell pepper and cook, uncovered, on high for 2 minutes, until softened. Stir in the mushrooms, flour, mustard, and pepper. Cook on high for 1 minute, stirring once. Gently stir in the milk. Cook on high for 3–4 minutes, stirring after 2 minutes, until the sauce boils and thickens. Stir in the cream and cook on high for 1 minute.

❖ Divide the pasta among warmed serving bowls and pour over the sauce. Serve immediately, sprinkled with the cheese.

tagliatelle
with ham and ricotta

serves 4–5

12 oz (375 g) tomato-flavored
tagliatelle

2 tablespoons butter

²⁄₃ cup (5 oz/155 g)
ricotta cheese

7 oz (220 g) ham, diced

6 green (spring) onions,
finely chopped

¼ teaspoon cayenne pepper

ground black pepper

7 oz (220 g) fresh mushrooms,
wiped clean and sliced

¾ cup (3 oz/90 g) grated
Parmesan cheese

¼ cup (2 fl oz/60 ml) cream

fresh parsley, for garnish
(optional)

❖ In a large saucepan of boiling salted water cook the pasta until al dente. Drain and cover to keep warm.

❖ Melt the butter in a 4–8 cup (1–2 qt/1–2 l) microwave-safe dish or casserole on high (100%) for 2 minutes, until bubbling. Stir in the ricotta, ham, green onions, cayenne pepper, black pepper, mushrooms, and cheese. Cook on medium (50%) for 3–4 minutes, until the cheese melts.

❖ Add the mushroom mixture and cream to the hot pasta and fold through until combined. Serve garnished with sprigs of parsley or chopped parsley, if desired.

pasta carbonara

Pasta carbonara, with its creamy combination of eggs, ham, and cheese, is a firm favorite. You can serve it with ribbon pasta, such as spaghetti, fettuccine, or linguine, if you prefer.

8 oz (250 g) pasta shells or other shaped pasta

½ cup (4 fl oz/125 ml) cream

3 eggs

¼ cup (1 oz/30 g) grated Parmesan cheese

2 tablespoons tomato purée

2 tablespoons white wine

1 tablespoon butter

2 cloves garlic, crushed

1 teaspoon dried oregano

6 green (spring) onions, roughly chopped

8 slices ham, cut into thin strips

2 tomatoes, peeled and chopped

chopped fresh parsley, for garnish

❖ In a large saucepan of boiling salted water cook the pasta until al dente. Drain and cover to keep warm.

❖ Meanwhile, lightly beat the cream, eggs, cheese, tomato purée, and wine in a medium jug. Set aside.

❖ Melt the butter in a 12-cup (3-qt/3-l) microwave-safe dish or casserole on high (100%) for 1 minute. Stir in the garlic, oregano, and green onions. Cover and cook on high for 2 minutes more. Stir in the ham and tomatoes. Cover and cook on medium-high (70%) for 4–5 minutes, stirring occasionally, until heated through.

❖ Add the pasta and egg mixture to the ham mixture and stir to combine. Cook on medium (50%) for 4–6 minutes, stirring every 2 minutes, until the sauce begins to thicken.

❖ Divide the mixture among warmed serving bowls. Serve immediately, garnished with chopped parsley.

peeling tomatoes

To peel tomatoes in the microwave, lightly slash or prick the skin, then place on a microwave-safe plate and heat on high (100%) for 10–40 seconds per tomato, depending on its ripeness, size, and firmness. Remove the skin with a small knife.

spinach tagliatelle
with salmon and broccoli

serves 4

8 oz (250 g) dried or 1 lb (500 g) fresh spinach tagliatelle

2 cups (4 oz/125 g) sliced broccoli florets

1 tablespoon butter

1 tablespoon all-purpose (plain) flour

½ cup (4 fl oz/125 ml) milk

½ cup (4 fl oz/125 ml) cream

1 clove garlic, crushed

salt and ground black pepper

4 oz (125 g) smoked salmon, cut into thin strips

❧ In a large saucepan of boiling salted water cook the pasta until al dente. Drain and cover to keep warm.

❧ Place the broccoli in a microwave-safe dish, cover, and cook on high (100%) for 1½–2 minutes or until just tender. Set aside, covered, while making the sauce.

❧ Melt the butter in a medium microwave-safe bowl on high for 30 seconds. Stir in the flour and cook for 1 minute, stirring after 30 seconds. Add the milk, cream, garlic, salt, and pepper. Whisk briskly to combine. Cook on high for 2 minutes, stirring often, until thickened. Stir in the salmon and broccoli and heat on high for about 30 seconds.

❧ Serve the sauce spooned over the hot pasta.

tomato and fennel
fettuccine

serves 4

8 oz (250 g) each of plain and spinach-flavored fresh fettuccine

1 medium onion, finely chopped

1 fennel bulb, thinly sliced

1 clove garlic, crushed

½ cup (4 fl oz/125 ml) water

1 tablespoon butter

1 lb (500 g) tomatoes, peeled and chopped

¼ cup (1⅓ oz/40 g) thinly sliced red bell pepper (capsicum)

2 tablespoons tomato paste

¼ cup (2 fl oz/60 ml) white wine or water

1 teaspoon dried basil

salt and ground black pepper

1 teaspoon sugar

❖ In a large saucepan of boiling salted water cook the pasta until al dente. Drain and cover to keep warm.

❖ Place the onion, fennel, garlic, water, and butter in a microwave-safe casserole and cook, covered, on high (100%) for 5 minutes, or until the onion and fennel are softened.

❖ Stir in the remaining ingredients and cook, covered, for 10 minutes on high, stirring halfway through cooking.

❖ Divide the pasta among warmed serving bowls and top with the sauce. Serve at once with crusty Italian bread, if desired.

creamy pork lasagna

serves 4

Lasagna with a twist. Quick and easy to prepare, this lasagna uses pork rather than the more traditional beef, and cream of chicken soup instead of white sauce. The result is a deliciously smooth and creamy lasagna.

1 tablespoon butter

1 onion, chopped

2 cups (8 oz/250 g) cooked, chopped pork

2 tablespoons all-purpose (plain) flour

¾ cup (6 fl oz/185 ml) hot chicken stock

½ teaspoon ground nutmeg

ground black pepper

3 oz (90 g) fresh mushrooms, wiped clean and finely shredded

1 bunch spinach leaves, washed and shredded

2 tablespoons cream

6 instant lasagne sheets

1 can (15 oz/470 g) condensed cream of chicken soup

1½ cups (6 oz/185 g) grated Cheddar cheese

❖ Melt the butter in a 12-cup (3-qt/3-l) microwave-safe dish or casserole on high (100%) for 1 minute. Stir in the onion, cover, and cook on high for 2 minutes. Add the pork, flour, stock, nutmeg, and pepper. Stir well, then cook on high for 3–4 minutes, stirring after 2 minutes, until the sauce boils and thickens. Stir in the mushrooms, spinach, and cream. Cover and cook on high for 3–4 minutes.

❖ Cover the base of a greased large, shallow microwave-safe baking dish with a layer of the pork mixture. Top with a layer of lasagna, then a third of the can of soup and a third of the cheese. Continue layering the pork mixture, lasagna, soup, and cheese until all the ingredients are used, finishing with a layer of cheese.

❖ Cook, uncovered, on medium (50%) for 20–25 minutes, or until the pasta is tender, the pork mixture heated through, and the cheese has melted.

❖ If desired, place briefly under a hot broiler (griller) to brown the top before serving.

tomato and bacon
ditalini

serves 4

8 oz (250 g) ditalini (short pasta tubes)

4 slices bacon, rind removed, fat trimmed

2 lb (1 kg) ripe tomatoes, peeled
and seeded, or 1 can (16 oz/500 g)
plum (Roma) tomatoes, undrained

1 clove garlic, crushed

1 medium onion, finely chopped

2 tablespoons olive oil

1 tablespoon chopped fresh oregano or
1/2 teaspoon dried oregano

1/2 green bell pepper (capsicum), stemmed,
seeded, and cut into thin strips

2 teaspoons sugar

1/2 cup (3 oz/90 g) sliced black olives

salt and ground black pepper

❖ In a large saucepan of boiling salted
water cook the pasta until al dente. Drain
and cover to keep warm.

❖ Place the bacon on a microwave-safe
plate between 4 sheets of paper towel.
Cook on high (100%) for 2 1/2–3 minutes,
or until cooked. Set aside to cool slightly,
then cut into pieces using kitchen scissors.

❖ Combine the remaining ingredients
and the bacon pieces in a 12-cup (3-qt/3-l)
microwave-safe casserole and cook,
uncovered, stirring occasionally, on high
for 15 minutes or until thickened. Spoon
over the pasta and serve with a green
salad, if desired.

fiery tomato penne

serves 4

13 oz (410 g) penne

1 tablespoon olive oil

2 cloves garlic, crushed

sliced fresh red chile, or
chile powder, to taste

½ cup (4 fl oz/125 ml)
tomato purée

ground black pepper

chopped fresh basil,
for garnish

❖ In a large saucepan of boiling salted water cook the pasta until al dente. Drain and cover to keep warm.

❖ Meanwhile, heat the oil in an 8-cup (2-qt/2-l) microwave-safe casserole, uncovered, on high (100%) for 2 minutes. Stir in the garlic and chile or chile powder. Cook, covered, on high for 1 minute, or until fragrant. Stir in the tomato purée and cook on high for 2 minutes, or until the sauce comes to a boil.

❖ Add the sauce to the pasta and toss to combine. Season with pepper, to taste, and serve sprinkled generously with basil.

ravioli
with tomato and garlic

serves 2–3

8 oz (250 g) fresh ravioli
(purchased or homemade)

2 tablespoons olive oil

2 cloves garlic, crushed

13 oz (410 g) canned
tomatoes, sieved

½ teaspoon ground allspice

ground black pepper

salt

✤ In a large saucepan of boiling salted water cook the pasta until al dente. Drain and cover to keep warm.

✤ Meanwhile, heat the oil in an 8-cup (2-qt/2-l) microwave-safe casserole on high (100%) for 2 minutes. Add the garlic and stir well to combine. Stir in the tomatoes, allspice, and pepper and cook, uncovered, on high for 6–8 minutes, or until the sauce comes to a boil, stirring halfway through cooking. Adjust the seasonings and add salt, if desired.

✤ Add the pasta to the tomato mixture and stir gently to combine. Cover and heat on medium-high (70%) until warmed through. Serve immediately with crusty Italian bread, if desired.

pasta marinara

serves 4

8 oz (250 g) fusilli
(pasta spirals)

2 tablespoons butter

1 clove garlic, crushed

2 tomatoes, peeled
and chopped

1 tablespoon tomato paste

¼ cup (2 fl oz/60 ml)
white wine

1 teaspoon chopped fresh basil

ground black pepper

1 tablespoon chopped
fresh parsley

1½ lb (750 g) marinara mix,
rinsed well, drained

❖ In a large saucepan of boiling salted water cook the pasta until al dente. Drain and cover to keep warm.

❖ Place the butter and garlic in an 8-cup (2-qt/2-l) microwave-safe dish or casserole and cook on high (100%) for 1 minute. Stir in the tomatoes, tomato paste, wine, basil, pepper, and parsley. Cook on high for 5 minutes, stirring well after 2 minutes. Transfer the tomato mixture to a blender or food processor and blend or process until smooth. Return to the dish or casserole and stir in the marinara mix. Heat on medium (50%) for 5–7 minutes or until warmed through. Spoon over the hot pasta and serve immediately.

macaroni casserole

serves 3–4

8 oz (250 g) macaroni

1/4 cup (2 oz/60 g) butter

1 onion, thinly sliced

1 clove garlic, crushed

3 oz (90 g) fresh mushrooms,
wiped clean and sliced

3 tomatoes, peeled
and chopped

1/4 cup (2 oz/60 g) tomato paste

8 oz (250 g) ham,
finely chopped

1/3 cup (2 1/2 fl oz/80 ml)
dry white wine

ground black pepper

chopped fresh parsley

grated Parmesan cheese

❖ In a large saucepan of boiling salted water cook the pasta until al dente. Drain and cover to keep warm.

❖ Meanwhile, melt the butter in a 12-cup (3-qt/3-l) casserole on high (100%) for 1 minute. Stir in the onion and garlic and cook, covered, on high for 2 minutes. Stir in the mushrooms, tomatoes, tomato paste, ham, wine, and pepper and cook on high for 4–5 minutes, or until heated through.

❖ Stir the pasta into the tomato mixture. Cover and heat on medium-high (70%) for 3–4 minutes, or until warmed through.

❖ Serve immediately, sprinkled with the parsley and cheese, and accompanied by fresh bread.

microwave macaroni cheese

serves 3–4

8 oz (250 g) macaroni

SAUCE

¼ cup (2 oz/60 g) butter

¼ cup (1 oz/30 g) all-purpose (plain) flour

2½ cups (20 fl oz/625 ml) milk

½ teaspoon English mustard

salt and ground black pepper

1½ cups (6 oz/185 g) grated tasty Cheddar cheese

pinch of paprika

❖ In a large saucepan of boiling salted water cook the pasta until al dente. Drain and cover to keep warm.

❖ Meanwhile, for the sauce, melt the butter in a 4-cup (1-qt/1-liter) microwave-safe bowl on high (100%) for 1 minute. Stir in the flour and cook, uncovered, for 1 minute on high, stirring halfway through cooking. Stir in the milk, mustard, salt, and pepper until well combined. Cook, uncovered, on high for 5–6 minutes, stirring every minute, or until thickened. Stir in a third of the cheese and heat on high for 30 seconds.

❖ Combine the pasta and sauce in a microwave-safe serving dish and sprinkle with the remaining cheese. Cook, uncovered, on high for 2–3 minutes, or until the cheese melts. Sprinkle with the paprika. Brown lightly under a hot broiler (griller), if desired. Serve at once.

part
Two

techniques

homemade
pasta

When there are so many delicious pasta varieties available ready made, why would you make your own? Simply because you can taste the difference. The result is more tender and delicate than packaged pasta, and will more fully absorb whatever sauce coats it. Homemade pasta requires the simplest of ingredients—flour, water, oil, salt, and eggs—and a minimum of mixing, kneading, and shaping. It is easy to prepare, whether by hand or with a simple hand-cranked pasta machine that clamps onto a kitchen counter or table. (These are available at most cookware stores.) Of course, you won't always have time to make your own, and a good-quality purchased fresh or dried pasta can be almost as satisfying as the pasta you prepare from scratch. If you wish to substitute fresh pasta for dried in any of the recipes in this book, use twice the weight of uncooked fresh pasta (homemade or purchased) as dried.

storage hints

dividing the dough After kneading, shape the dough into a round; do not roll out. Using a sharp knife, divide the round into fourths or whatever portion size is specified in the recipe.

freezing dough Wrap each portion airtight in plastic wrap. Then store in a freezer-safe container or in heavy-duty freezer bags. The dough will keep in the freezer for up to 8 months.

making pasta by hand

adding egg mixture to flour

Stir together flour and salt in a large mixing bowl. Make a well or depression in the center. In another bowl combine eggs, water, and oil and pour the liquid into the well in the flour mixture. Mix thoroughly with a wooden spoon.

kneading by hand

Lightly flour a work surface. To knead, curve your fingers over the edge of the dough and pull it toward you. Then push down and away with the heel of your hand. Give the dough a quarter turn, fold it toward you, and repeat the process. Cover and let rest for 10 minutes before rolling out.

rolling the dough

Divide the dough into recipe-sized portions, usually in fourths. Set one portion on a floured work surface. Flatten with a rolling pin to about a 1-inch (2.5-cm) thickness. Cover the remaining dough with a kitchen towel or plastic wrap so it won't dry out, or freeze for later use as described on page 300.

Continue rolling the dough until it is $1/16$ inch (2 mm) thick. A one-quarter portion will roll out to a square that is about 12 x 12 inches (30 x 30 cm).

After rolling, let the dough rest, uncovered, for 20 minutes so the surface will dry slightly. Shape, slice, or fill according to recipe directions.

making pasta
by machine

When pasta dough is mixed in a food processor, then rolled to paper thinness in a manual pasta maker, the whole process becomes almost effortless.

As usual, the food processor does its job quickly. Monitor the dough at every step. If you don't have a pasta machine, you can knead food processor dough with your hands and roll it out with a rolling pin as described on page 301. However, the hand-cranked pasta machine is relatively inexpensive compared to most home appliances and is small enough to store out of sight when not in use. If you make pasta often, it might be a sensible purchase because it takes almost all of the work out of kneading and rolling.

processing dry ingredients

Place flour, salt, and eggs in the work bowl of a food processor. Cover and process with a pulsing action until the mixture is the consistency of cornmeal. This happens very quickly, so don't overprocess.

adding liquid

Put water, oil, and any other liquid in a measuring cup with a lip. With the processor running, slowly pour the liquid through the feed tube into the work bowl. The flour mixture will begin to form a cohesive mass.

forming a ball

Continue processing the mixture just until the dough forms a ball. Stop once or twice to scrape down the sides of the work bowl so all the ingredients are incorporated into the dough. Remove from the work bowl, pat into a ball, cover with a kitchen towel or plastic wrap, and let rest at room temperature for 10 minutes.

kneading in pasta machine

Divide the dough into 4 portions or as directed in the recipe. Cover unused dough or freeze (see page 300). Slightly flatten one portion with your hands and feed through the rollers at the lowest setting, with the rollers wide apart. Fold in half or thirds, give a quarter turn, and run through the same setting. Repeat until dough is smooth and no longer tears.

rolling in pasta machine

Once the sheet of dough feeds through the rollers easily and looks smooth and silky, almost rubbery, without rough spots, turn to the next setting. If you really have to crank hard, go back to a wider setting.

Lightly flour the dough, fold, give a quarter turn, and pass through the machine again. Repeat folding, turning, and rolling at increasingly higher (narrower) settings until the dough is the proper texture and thickness, usually ⅛ inch (3 mm) thick. Then slice, shape, or fill as required.

See pages 306–308 for recipes for plain and flavored pasta dough.

basic equipment

To prepare pasta by machine, you will need a small bowl, a measuring cup, a rubber spatula, and a food processor to mix the ingredients, and a hand-cranked pasta maker to knead and roll the dough.

basic pasta dough

**makes 4 portions pasta
(1 lb/500 g total)**

**This simple dough (or Semolina
Pasta Dough and its variations,
pages 306–307) can be used for every
recipe in this book that calls for fresh
pasta. Although quick to prepare,
to save more time you can make the
dough ahead and freeze (see
the tip box on page 300 for freezing
directions). To substitute fresh pasta
in a recipe that specifies dried, use
twice as much fresh pasta as dried.**

2 cups (8 oz/250 g) all-purpose (plain) flour

1/2 teaspoon salt

2 eggs, lightly beaten

1/3 cup (2 1/2 fl oz/80 ml) water

1 teaspoon olive oil or cooking oil

1/3 cup (1 1/2 oz/45 g) all-purpose (plain)
flour, extra, for dusting

❖ In a large mixing bowl stir together the
2 cups (8 oz/250 g) flour and the salt.
Make a well in the center.

❖ In a small mixing bowl stir together the
eggs, water, and oil. Add to the flour and
mix well.

❖ Sprinkle a work surface with the 1/3 cup
(1 1/2 oz/45 g) flour. (Spinach, whole-wheat,
herb, or tomato variations may not require

the addition of any or all of this flour.) Turn dough out onto the floured work surface. Knead until dough is smooth and elastic (8–10 minutes). Cover and let rest for 10 minutes.

❖ Divide dough into fourths. On the lightly floured work surface, roll each fourth into a 12-inch (30-cm) square about 1/16 inch (2 mm) thick. Let stand about 20 minutes, or until slightly dry. Or, if using a pasta machine, pass each fourth of dough through the machine, according to manufacturer's directions, until 1/16 inch (2 mm) thick. Shape or stuff as desired, or as directed in recipe.

❖ For ribbon pasta, roll up the pasta sheet to form a firm roll. Using a sharp knife, slice the roll to form strips of pasta. To dry ribbons, hang pasta from a pasta-drying rack or clothes hanger, or toss with flour, shape into loose bundles, and place on a floured baking sheet. Let dry overnight or until completely dry. Place in an airtight container and refrigerate up to 3 days. Or, dry the pasta for at least 1 hour. Seal it in a freezer bag or container. Freeze for up to 8 months.

recipe variations

herb pasta Prepare pasta as directed, except add 1 teaspoon dried basil, marjoram, or sage, crushed, to flour mixture.

spinach pasta Prepare pasta as directed, except decrease the water to 3 tablespoons and add 1/3 cup (2 1/2 oz/75 g) cooked, well drained, very finely chopped spinach to the egg mixture.

whole-wheat pasta Prepare pasta as directed, except substitute whole-wheat (wholemeal) flour for the all-purpose flour.

tomato pasta Prepare pasta as directed, except substitute tomato paste for the water.

semolina
pasta dough

makes 1 lb (500 g)

1 cup (4 oz/125 g) unsifted all-purpose
(plain) flour

1 cup (5 oz/155 g) semolina

1 good pinch salt

3 eggs, lightly beaten

1 tablespoon olive oil

water, as needed

by hand

❖ Place the flour, semolina, and salt in
a large mixing bowl. Mix thoroughly. Make
a well in the center and add the eggs and
the oil. Work the liquid very thoroughly into
the flour, adding a little water if necessary.

❖ When all the liquid is incorporated,
bring the mixture together to form a ball.

❖ On a floured work surface, knead dough
for 10 minutes until smooth and elastic.
Wrap in plastic wrap and let rest for 1 hour.

❖ Divide dough into fourths. Roll out each
portion to the desired thickness and length.

❖ Roll up the pasta sheet to form a firm
roll. Using a sharp knife, slice the roll to
form strips of pasta. Dry as instructed on
page 305, or freeze.

by machine

❖ Place eggs and oil in the food processor. Process to mix. Add the flour and semolina and process until the mixture forms a ball.

❖ On a lightly floured surface, knead the dough until smooth and elastic. Divide into four equal quantities. Hand roll each into a rectangular shape. Set the pasta machine on its widest setting and roll pasta several times, folding it in half after each pass.

❖ Continue rolling the pasta dough through the machine, adjusting the machine to progressively finer settings with each pass. Dust the dough with a little extra flour if necessary. Roll out to the desired thickness.

❖ To cut the pasta into fettuccine or a finer width, roll the dough through the appropriate attachment for the desired width. Or, roll up the pasta sheet to form a firm roll. Using a sharp knife, slice the roll to form strips of pasta of the desired width.

recipe variations

whole wheat pasta
1¼ cups (5 oz/155 g) all-purpose (plain) flour
1¼ cups (5 oz/155 g) whole-wheat (wholemeal) flour
3 eggs
Proceed as for plain pasta. A little water may be necessary to bind it together.

fresh herb pasta A single herb or a mixture of herbs can be used. The herbs must be washed, thoroughly dried, and finely chopped. Add ¼ cup of fresh herbs of your choice to the flour and proceed as for plain pasta dough.

spinach pasta To the eggs, add ¼ cup (2 oz/60 g) of finely chopped, cooked spinach that has been squeezed to remove all excess moisture. Add the eggs and spinach to the flour, then mix well. Proceed as for plain pasta dough. It may be necessary to work in a little extra flour if the mixture is too moist.

cooking pasta

Even the best pasta, whether fresh or dried, can be ruined if improperly cooked. The steps below explain this elementary but critical technique.

Always use a large saucepan so that the pasta can circulate freely in vigorously boiling water with room to expand as it cooks. If the saucepan is too small, the pasta will stick together; you also risk an overflow of the scalding, bubbling liquid. A pasta saucepan with a strainer insert is practical: It is the right size and lets you drain off the water with very little effort because the water flows back into the pan when you lift the insert. Salt may be added to the water for flavor and oil helps keep pasta from sticking, but neither is a must.

Fresh pasta never needs more than a few minutes to cook. Dried ribbons and shapes take longer, anywhere from 8–15 minutes (check the package for recommended cooking times). Both types are done when the texture is tender but still slightly chewy and no traces of raw pasta remain when you bite into a piece—a quality described as "al dente." Drain, then transfer to a warmed serving bowl and toss immediately with sauce or use as directed in the recipe. A pasta rake in wood, metal, or plastic works best for tossing and serving pasta.

adding pasta to water

Fill a large saucepan with 3 qt (3 l) of water for every 4–8 oz (125–250 g) of pasta. Bring to a vigorous, rolling boil. Add 1 teaspoon of salt and 1 tablespoon of oil, if desired. Then add the pasta, a little at a time, so the water stays at a boil. Stir to prevent the pasta from sticking.

stirring occasionally

While the pasta is cooking, stir occasionally with a wooden spoon or pasta rake to keep the strands or pieces from sticking together as they swirl around in the water.

testing for doneness

Near the end of cooking time, taste often to check for doneness. Pasta is ready when the texture is tender but still slightly firm, or "al dente." Don't let the cooked pasta sit in the cooking water or it will overcook and become mushy.

two ways to drain

removing drainer insert

If using a pasta saucepan with an insert, lift up the insert by the handles (protect your hands with oven mitts, if necessary). The cooking water will drain back into the pan.

draining in a colander

Set a colander in the sink. If using a standard saucepan without a drainer insert, pour the pasta and water into the colander as soon as the pasta is done. Lift up the colander (be careful of steam burns) and give it a bit of a shake to shed excess water from the pasta.

nutritional information

Per portion plain pasta: 292 calories, 10 g protein, 51 g carbohydrate, 4 g total fat (1 g saturated), 107 mg cholesterol, 300 mg sodium, 102 mg potassium.

glossary

artichokes

The artichoke is the edible bud of a tall, thistle-like plant. Only the fleshy base of the leaves and the meaty bottom of the bud are eaten; the rest of the leaf and the fuzzy interior choke are discarded. Artichokes are sold fresh year-round, in sizes ranging from very small to very large; they are also available frozen, canned, and marinated. Select compact, heavy globes with tightly closed leaves. Store in a plastic bag in the refrigerator for up to 4 days.

asparagus

This tender stalk with a tightly closed bud is prized for its delicate flavor and subtle hue (white asparagus, a delicacy, is not commonly available). Crisp, straight, firm stalks with a tight cap are best. Wrap in damp paper towels and store in a plastic bag in the refrigerator for up to 4 days.

basil

With its affinity for sauces and tomato-based dishes, it isn't surprising to find basil in many pasta recipes. Intensely aromatic, fresh basil arrives in summer, when tomatoes are at their peak; dried basil may be found on the spice shelf year-round. Store freshly cut stems in a glass with a little water, covered with plastic wrap, in the refrigerator for up to 2 days.

bell peppers

Also known as capsicum, these colorful, crunchy vegetable–fruits are related to chiles, although they are far milder in taste. They change color as they ripen, from green to orange, yellow, red, or purple. They can be eaten raw, added to salads, or cooked, when they become much sweeter and softer. Store in a plastic bag in the refrigerator for up to 1 week.

broccoli

Both the rigid green stalks and the tightly packed dark-green or purplish-green heads (also called florets) are edible. Choose firm stalks and closed heads with deep color and no yellow areas. Store in a plastic bag in the refrigerator for up to 4 days.

cannellini beans

Also known as white kidney beans, these are mild-flavored and meaty, and are available dried or canned. Great Northern (white haricot) beans can be substituted.

capers

Capers are the pickled flower buds of a Mediterranean bush, and add a piquant note to foods. Most markets stock them in jars with other condiments. Store opened jars in the refrigerator. Before using, drain off their preserving liquid.

carrots

Choose firm, bright-orange carrots; avoid those that are droopy or have cracks or dry spots. Store them in a plastic bag, tops removed, in the refrigerator for up to 2 weeks. Either peel or scrub carrots before using. Tiny baby carrots are actually a separate variety, prized for their delicate flavor and charming appearance. Store them as you would regular carrots.

cheeses

The following cheeses often appear in pasta dishes:

Mascarpone is rich and buttery, a cross between cream cheese and sour cream.

Mozzarella is pliable and stringy, and is used in baked dishes and salads.

Parmesan is a hard and crumbly grating

cheese with a nutty flavor. It is used, usually shaved, shredded, or grated, as the finishing touch on many pasta dishes. *Ricotta* is mild and semisweet, with a soft, creamy texture.

Romano is similar to Parmesan, but is sharper in taste.

Note: Storage varies with the type of cheese, but all cheeses must be wrapped well and refrigerated to stay fresh.

chives

When snipped into little pieces, the long, hollow green leaves of this herb add bright color and a mild onion flavor to many dishes. Fresh chives should not be wilted or damaged. Wrap in damp paper towels and store in a plastic bag in the refrigerator for up to 4 days.

fava beans

Also known as broad beans, these are large, slightly flattened, green or light-brown beans. When they are very young, the whole pods can be eaten, but usually they are shelled like peas. Fava beans are available fresh, frozen, and dried.

fennel

With its tubular stalks and feathery leaves, this bulbous, creamy-white to pale-green vegetable resembles celery, but its flavor hints of licorice. Fresh fennel is delicious raw or cooked; dried fennel seeds are used as a seasoning. Select bulbs that are free of cracks or brown spots. Store in a plastic bag in the refrigerator for up to 4 days.

garlic

A bulb with a papery outer skin, a head of garlic is composed of numerous small cloves. Garlic may be used as a savory seasoning for every savory course of a meal. It is aromatic and almost bitter when raw, but becomes delicate and sweet when cooked. Fresh garlic should be plump and firm. Store whole garlic bulbs in a cool, dark, dry place.

ginger

The rhizome, or underground stem, of a semitropical plant, fresh ginger is a pungent seasoning with a lively, hot flavor and peppery aroma. Select stems that are firm and heavy, never shrivelled, with taut, glossy skin. Wrap in a paper towel and store in the refrigerator for up to 2 days. For longer storage, wrap airtight and freeze the unpeeled root.

kale

A member of the cabbage family, kale has ruffled dark-green leaves and tastes similar to its cabbage relatives. It is eaten fresh or cooked, or can be used as a decorative garnish. Wash the leaves under cold running water, dry well, and then store in a paper towel-lined plastic bag in the refrigerator for up to 3 days.

olive oil

A staple of Mediterranean cooking, olive oil imparts a clean, fruity flavor and golden-to-green color to salad dressings, grilled bread, and pasta sauces. Use extra-virgin oils, from the first pressing, for cold dishes. For sauces, use milder oils that can stand up to heat. Store in a dark spot away from heat for 6 months, or in the refrigerator for a year. (Chilled oil may become thick and cloudy; let it warm to room temperature before using.)

oregano

Packed with robust flavor and aroma, oregano is a favorite herb of Italian and Greek cooks. Select bright-green fresh oregano with firm stems. Look for dried whole or ground oregano with other spices. Refrigerate fresh oregano in a plastic bag for up to 3 days.

pancetta

Mild, spicy-sweet Italian pancetta is rarely smoked, unlike regular bacon, although it is usually seasoned with pepper. It is sold in specialty markets in a roll rather than in a flat slab. Store it, well wrapped, in the refrigerator for several weeks.

parsley

Widely used for cooking and as a garnish, parsley has such a clean, refreshing flavor that it is sometimes enjoyed as an after-meal digestive. Curly-leaf parsley is mild, while flat-leaf (Italian) parsley is more pungent. Select healthy, lively looking bunches. To store, rinse under cold running water, shake dry, then wrap in paper towels and keep in a plastic bag in the refrigerator for up to 1 week.

prosciutto

This spicy, air-dried Italian ham is either eaten raw in paper-thin slices or cooked as part of a recipe. Top-quality *prosciutto di Parma* is imported from Italy, but many excellent domestic varieties are available. (Italian delicatessens and most specialty markets will stock both.) Wrap well and store in the refrigerator for several weeks.

squash

Slender, soft-skinned green and yellow zucchini, straight and crookneck squashes, and pattypan squashes are classified as "summer" vegetables, although many are sold year-round. Select heavy, well-shaped squash without cracks or bruises. Store for up to 4 days in the refrigerator.

tomatoes

Although they are botanically a fruit, tomatoes are eaten as a vegetable. Oval-shaped plum tomatoes (also called Italian or Roma) are thick and meaty, with less juice and smaller seeds than other varieties, which makes them ideal for sauces. They are sold fresh, or in cans sometimes flavored with basil and other seasonings. Other market forms include stewed tomatoes, cooked with celery, onions, and seasonings; tomato paste, a highly concentrated purée; and sweet, chewy sun-dried tomatoes, either plain or packed in oil.

index

Page numbers in italics refer to photographs.

a note on
measurements

U.S. cup measurements are
used throughout this book.
Slight adjustments may
need to be made to
quantities if Imperial or
metric measures are used.

....

acknowledgments

Weldon Owen wishes to
thank the following people
for their assistance in the
production of this book:
Lynn Cole (proofreading);
Angela Handley (editorial
assistance); Nancy Sibtain
(indexing).

gnocchirav
tagliatellepe
fettuccinepe
lasagnacann
spaghettich
orecchiettes